Thelma,

May God [...] and bring you peace during this time of loss.

We're always here for you if you are ever in need of anything.

Prayerfully yours,
Ed Bacon

WHEN GRIEF IS YOUR CONSTANT COMPANION

WHEN *Grief* IS YOUR CONSTANT COMPANION

God's Grace for a Woman's Heartache

Carolyn Rhea

New Hope Publishers

Birmingham, Alabama

New Hope Publishers
P. O. Box 12065
Birmingham, AL 35202-2065
www.newhopepubl.com

Library of Congress Cataloging-in-Publication Data
Rhea, Carolyn.
When grief is your constant companion : God's grace for a woman's heartache / Carolyn Rhea.
p. cm.
ISBN 1-56309-748-6
1.Bereavement-Religious aspects-Christianity. 2. Consolation. I. Title.
BV4905.3 .R48 2003
242'.4—dc21
2002012422

Unless otherwise noted, Scripture quotations are taken from The Holy Bible, King James Version.

Scripture quotations marked (NIV) are taken from the HOLY BIBLE, NEW INTERNATIONAL VERSION®. NIV®. Copyright©1973, 1978, 1984 by International Bible Society. Used by permission of Zondervan. All rights reserved.

Scripture quotations marked (NKJV) are taken from the New King James Version. Copyright © 1982 by Thomas Nelson, Inc. Used by permission. All rights reserved.

Scriptures marked (TEV) are taken from the Good News Bible in Today's English Version—Second Edition, Copyright © 1992 by American Bible Society. Used by Permission.

Cover design by Steve Diggs & Friends

ISBN: 1-56309-748-6

N034108 • 0103 • 9M1

*To My Beloved Claude
Who Awaits My Coming*

TABLE OF CONTENTS

PRELUDE:
GRIEF STRIKES
MY LIFE

A fierce storm lashed West Palm Beach during the pre-dawn hours of Wednesday, September 19, 1990. Startled by a brilliant flash of lightning followed almost instantly by house-shaking thunder, I awoke. For a long while I lay awake, thinking, "What an awful storm! Lightning must have struck nearby. If only Claude were here." But my husband, Dr. Claude Rhea, couldn't be with me at the time. He was in Paris, France, on a business trip.

Later that day, I was chatting with a friend after I spoke at a luncheon at Palm Beach Atlantic College (now Palm Beach Atlantic University), where my husband was president.

"Carolyn, have you seen the tree that was struck by lightning early this morning?" she inquired.

"Which tree?" I asked. "One here on campus?"

"Yes, the huge ficus tree outside Claude's office."

Of course I wanted to see it! How Claude loved that tree! To him it was symbolic of Palm Beach Atlantic College. When he accepted the presidency of that college eight and one half years earlier, the old ficus tree stood valiantly among the old campus buildings. During Claude's time there, several new buildings were constructed. He had the majestic ficus tree dug up and transplanted (by crane!) just outside his office.

When my friend and I reached the site of the fallen tree, nothing remained. During the early morning storm, lightning had splintered its frame in an instant. Removing it quickly was imperative, for it had become a traffic hazard. Freshly-placed flagstones created a virgin path across the ground so recently sheltered by Claude's beloved ficus tree. For a short while, my friend and I stood there talking about Claude's fallen tree.

Meanwhile, my husband, Claude, was waiting in Charles de Gaulle Airport near Paris, France, for a flight to London. Suddenly, he experienced great difficulty breathing and was rushed to the emergency clinic at the airport. Doctors tried in vain to save his life. He died of heart failure there in the airport at 8:25 P.M. Paris time (2:25 P.M. West Palm Beach time).

The last words he spoke were these: "Tell Carolyn I love her."

My friend and I did not know that while we were standing at the site of the fallen tree, my beloved husband of thirty-nine years was dying in France. Never again would his loving presence shelter me, his wife and helpmate. My life was changed forever. I was now a widow, wandering alone in the wilderness of grief.

> Like lightning, grief strikes my life.
> Its piercing impact momentarily paralyzes
> My mind, but soon the reality of loss
> Shatters the numbness with torrents
> Of despair.

This sketch by Ruth Robinson shows the ficus tree outside Claude's office.

LIFE TOGETHER

The shock was devastating. How could it be that my Claude was dead? Only a few weeks earlier, we had joyfully celebrated our thirty-ninth wedding anniversary. We recalled how God had brought us together in His own wonderful way and time.

Hawaii was the setting for our romance! We were college students doing mission work in Hawaii during the summer of 1949. We fell in love as we worked together in Vacation Bible Schools, youth revivals, and other assignments. With a straight face, Claude insisted that a coconut hit him on the head and that I snared him while he was knocked out! We were married two years later, August 26, 1951.

Claude had a glorious tenor voice. After serving in World War II, Claude had entered William Jewell College in Liberty, Missouri. His majors changed from pre-med to history and then to music. When he finally recognized his God-given musical talent, he sought to honor God through it. At first he considered an operatic career, but God led him into a broader ministry of music through churches, concerts, recordings, foreign missions, and teaching.

In the foreword to Claude's autobiography, *With My Song I Will Praise Him*, Dr. Baker James Cauthen speaks of the impact of Claude's music: "Those who hear Claude Rhea sing are deeply moved not only by the beauty of his voice and the excellence of his technical performance but by a remarkable spiritual quality of depth, sincerity, and love." Claude was an excellent choral director, too. Especially gifted in leading congregational singing, he inspired people to express to God their love, faith, and praise with heart and song! He led the music and sang solos at Southern Baptist Conventions, Baptist World Alliance meetings, and evangelistic crusades, and he gave concerts here in the United States and in many countries throughout the world.

During his ministry of music, he made five recordings. He served as minister of music in a number of Baptist churches, as dean of the school of church music at New Orleans Baptist Theological Seminary, as vice-president of Houston Baptist University in Texas, as music consultant for the Baptist Foreign Mission Board in Virginia, as dean of the school of music at Samford University in Alabama, and finally as president of Palm Beach Atlantic College, where he was serving at the time of his death.

My own life—primarily as homemaker but sometimes as writer, speaker, and teacher—had revolved around Claude and his work in each successive ministry to which God called him.

My Claude

Claude was always a visionary. In every ministry in which he served, he dared to dream great dreams that would honor God. He lived faith as a verb, too—not just as a noun. Often I heard him say, "I *faith* You, God!" His favorite Bible verse was Isaiah 43:19: "Watch for the new thing [God is] going to do. . . . It's happening already. You can see it now!"(TEV). Those words are inscribed on his gravestone.

Claude was an eternal optimist with boundless faith in God, joy in his soul, a song in his heart, a spring in his step, and a word of encouragement for everyone. We were a good balance for each other: he, an optimist and I, a realist. My realism, I confess, bordered upon pessimism at times. But I caught most of his dreams and gladly worked to help him achieve them.

Life together was good!

We had our differences, of course; and we made many

mistakes. We had our faults, failures, and fiascos; but we were blessed with love! Life brought challenges and problems, but it also brought great joy. We experienced the joys and trials of rearing three children: Claude III (whom we call C3), Randall (Randy), and Margaret (Meg). Together, Claude and I wrote two books of original children's songs—*A Child's Life in Song* and *Sing While You Grow*—inspired by life with our children.

My beloved Claude also knew pain and suffering. He had had several brushes with death during our marriage, and God spared him each time. But in His wise and perfect will, God did not spare Claude that September day, 1990, in Paris, France.

LIFE ALONE

In the shock of losing my beloved Claude, I found myself wandering through a dark wilderness of grief. Ironically, we were living on Wilderness Road at the time of his death. The comfort of family helped, but our three children lived in distant states. Only Claude's 92-year-old mother, for whom I was responsible, lived near. Legally blind, she resided in an assisted-living facility. The comfort of friends, both near and far, helped too.

But my greatest comfort was my Christian faith. Though feeble at times, my faith failed not. It sustained me in my bereavement. I experienced anew my Heavenly Father's love for me personally. Bereft of my beloved earthly companion, my broken heart became more conscious of God's loving presence. Grief stilled all of life's busy distractions. I was truly alone with God. "The LORD is nigh unto them that are of a broken heart" (Psalm 34:18). What a *wonderful* promise! My Heavenly Father was near!

In the stillness of my broken heart, I sensed God's under-girding love and Christ's readiness to lead me through this wilderness of grief. Through the years I had trusted Him as Savior and Lord. I could trust Him now. He was the Way! The security of my faith in Christ strengthened me. His loving presence guided me. The Holy Spirit helped comfort me.

God's eternal Word spoke to my mind and heart. The Scriptures are a vital part of my sojourn in the wilderness of grief. "For whatsoever things were written aforetime were written for our learning, that we through patience and comfort of the scriptures might have hope." (Romans 15:4) How true! As Christ opened to me the Scriptures, they ministered to my need for comfort, courage, strength, and hope.

Reading books about other widows' grief helped me feel less overwhelmed as I discovered some common experiences of widowhood. Reading the advice of grief counselors helped also.

Penning my own pilgrimage brought comfort, too. Then, as I began to reach out to new widows whom I met, I felt their pain. I wanted to become a comforter. I remembered Claude's fallen ficus tree.

BECOMING A COMFORTER

The flash that struck thy tree—no more
To shelter thee—lets heaven's blue floor
Shine where it never shone before.
The cry wrung from thy spirit's pain
May echo in some far-off plain,
And guide a wanderer home again.
—Author Unknown

"Blessed be God, even the Father of our Lord Jesus Christ, the Father of mercies, and the God of all comfort: Who comforteth us in all our tribulation, that we may be able to comfort them which are in trouble, by the comfort wherewith we ourselves are comforted of God." —2 Corinthians 1:3, 4

Sharing My Journey

Are you a grieving widow, too?

If so, I pray that somewhere within this book you will find some degree of comfort. Did your husband have a long and painful illness? Did you have to endure the agony of watching him suffer greatly and die slowly? Did that experience make it easier for you to give him back to God? Or did it embitter you? Did his illness give you time and opportunity to prepare for separation? To express your love for each other? To make plans together? To pray together? To affirm your Christian faith? To experience God's peace even in the face of death? If so, you have priceless memories upon which to draw!

Or did your husband die quite suddenly, as mine did? The shock of Claude's death was devastating. He was only sixty-two. There was no time to talk about his death and its crushing impact upon my life. No time to discuss funeral arrangements. No time to say, "I love you!" No time to utter a final farewell: "Goodbye, my darling. I'll see you in heaven."

Mercifully, God spared my Claude from prolonged pain and suffering. But God did not spare me from the traumatic shock of losing my beloved so suddenly and so far away. My Heavenly Father did not abandon me in my grief. Underneath were His everlasting arms, and Christ my Savior taught me to walk by faith through the wilderness. The Holy Spirit brought consolation.

I found God's grace—unmerited love and divine assistance—to be sufficient for my journey.

Perhaps, after losing your husband, you returned to your job and your routine, staying busy with work, family, and friends. Perhaps you were already secure in your personal identity. If so, you were blessed. My life and work were closely merged with my husband's. After his death, I faced the struggle of finding my own "separate self." I've had to restructure my life in God's will and seek the new ministries He envisions for me now that I am alone.

"Thou tellest my wanderings; put thou my tears into thy bottle: are they not in thy book?" —*Psalm 56:8*

This book recounts my journey through the wilderness of grief. Under each heading, you will find my personal outpourings of grief, along with God's outpourings of comfort through Scripture—His eternal Word, which speaks to me at my point of need. I now have a deeper appreciation of the scope of the Bible: complaint and praise; guilt and forgiveness; failure and redemption; fear and courage; weakness and strength; grief and joy; suffering and healing; loss and gain; death and resurrection. I can identify with Job's anguish, Elijah's depression, and David's cries for help.

My grieving was done in the presence of God. Like Hannah of old, "I have . . . poured out my soul before the LORD . . . for out of the abundance of my complaint and grief have I spoken" (1 Samuel 1:15, 16).

My Heavenly Father, who created me and already knows all about me, listened compassionately and communicated His unfailing love and His promise of assistance—what wondrous grace! These outpourings of grief and comfort, which I am now sharing with you, are my innermost thoughts, written from my heart.

Each widow's journey through grief is uniquely her own. There is no absolute timetable for "recovery." Grief is intensely personal, and each widow grieves in her own way and time—whether months or years. In marriage, the quality of the relationship, the difficulty of circumstances, the depth of commitment, the degree of separate identity, the strength of spiritual convictions, and other variables affect our grief experience. We cope with our loss in different ways. We have traveled similar paths, though not identical ones. You will not be able to identify with all of my painful journey, nor can I relate fully to yours.

Nevertheless, grief has some common denominators. Perhaps you will glimpse a few as you wander with me through this wilderness of grief. My prayer is that God might use the pages of this book—my own grief experience and the Scriptures—to help comfort you.

In turn, you, too, can become a comforter.

Lord, give me eyes that I may see,
Lest I as people will,
Should pass someone's Calvary
And think it just a hill.
—Author Unknown

SECTION ONE

ACQUAINTED WITH GRIEF

ACQUAINTED WITH GRIEF

OUTPOURINGS OF GRIEF

I am acquainted with grief.
Intimately acquainted.

My beloved is dead.

Grief is my constant companion.
My unshakable companion.
Tear-blind, I stumble through this wilderness of
grief.

You are acquainted with grief, Lord Jesus.
Man of Sorrows, draw near, I pray,
And journey with me
Even as You joined the two
On the road to Emmaus long ago.
They were grieving also
And didn't understand Your death.

So You walked with them
And illumined the Scriptures.

And when You blessed the broken bread,
They beheld You as Risen Lord!
Open to me the Scriptures, please,
Concerning death and resurrection.
Strengthen my faith in Thee, Lord,
And in God's eternal promises.

Because You conquered death,
My beloved lives on in immortality
In Your promised land of heaven,
And I shall join him there.

But during this earthly "meanwhile"
Of brokenness and pain, Lord,
Please resurrect my shattered self.
Help me walk with faith and courage

Through this awful wilderness of grief,
Knowing that You are with me
And that You *are the way*.

OUTPOURINGS
OF COMFORT

"Daughter, be of good comfort." —*Matthew 9:22*

"I will not leave you comfortless: I will come to you." —*John 14:18*

"And, behold, two of them went . . . to a village called Emmaus. . . . And they talked together of all these things which had happened [Jesus' death, burial, and resurrection]. And it came to pass, that . . . Jesus himself drew near, and went with them. . . . And beginning at Moses and all the prophets, he expounded unto them in all the Scriptures the things concerning himself." —*Luke 24:13–15, 27*

"Jesus saith unto him, I am the way." —*John 14:6*

"And I [Jesus] will pray the Father, and he shall give you another Comforter, that he may abide with you for ever; even the Spirit of Truth." —*John 14:16–17*

"The Spirit of the Lord GOD is upon me . . . he hath sent me to bind up the brokenhearted . . . to comfort all that mourn . . . to give unto them beauty for ashes, the oil of joy for mourning."
—*Isaiah 61:1–3*

"The Lord is nigh unto them that are of a broken heart." —*Psalm 34:18*

"Blessed are they that mourn: for they shall be comforted." —*Matthew 5:4*

"Be of good courage, and he shall strengthen your heart, all ye that hope in the LORD." —*Psalm 31:24*

"Be strong in the grace that is in Christ Jesus."
—*2 Timothy 2:1*

"For we walk by faith, not by sight."
—*2 Corinthians 5:7*

CELEBRATION

OUTPOURINGS
OF GRIEF

Lord, the two memorial services today
For my beloved
Were ones of celebration.

First, as college family, we celebrated
His vision and leadership.
Then with family and friends from near and far
We celebrated the blessing of his life.

We celebrated with music he loved—
Music which proclaimed
Thy greatness,
Thy love,
Thy grace,
Thy peace.
My mind still hears the haunting bagpipe strains
Of "Amazing Grace."

We celebrated with testimonies
About his great faith,
His joy and optimism,
His ministry of encouragement,
His ministry through music,
His ministry through missions,
His ministry through education,
His ministry to his family.

We celebrated with the Scriptures
Your promise of resurrection,
Your promise of heaven,
Your words of comfort.

We celebrated with prayers
Of gratitude for his life,
Of trust in Thee and Thy ongoing will.
Yes, we celebrated his wonderful life.

But now the celebration has ended.
I am here alone,
And my heart is breaking.

OUTPOURINGS
OF COMFORT

"Precious in the sight of the LORD is the death of his saints." —*Psalm 116:15*

"And I heard a voice from heaven saying unto me, Write, Blessed are the dead which die in the Lord from henceforth: Yea, saith the Spirit, that they may rest from their labors; and their works do follow them." —*Revelation 14:13*

"His lord said unto him, Well done, good and faithful servant . . . enter thou into the joy of thy lord." —*Matthew 25:23*

"Be thou faithful unto death, and I will give thee a crown of life." —*Revelation 2:10*

"Christ shall be magnified in my body, whether it be by life, or by death." —*Philippians 1:20*

"For me to live is Christ, and to die is gain."
—*Philippians 1:21*

"I have fought a good fight, I have finished my course, I have kept the faith: henceforth there is laid up for me a crown of righteousness, which the Lord, the righteous judge, shall give me at that day: and not to me only, but unto all them also that love his appearing." —*2 Timothy 4:7–8*

"Eye hath not seen, nor ear heard . . . the things which God hath prepared for them that love him." —*1 Corinthians 2:9*

"I will make thee . . . a joy of many generations."
—*Isaiah 60:15*

"The memory of the just is blessed."
—*Proverbs 10:7*

BURIAL

OUTPOURINGS OF GRIEF

My beloved is buried, Father.

His earthly body—
He whom I knew and loved so well—
Lies in the grave,
Forever beyond my mortal reach.

Never again will I rush into his arms
And feel his warm embrace.
Or sit beside him and pour out my heart.
Or lie beside him and snuggle close.
Or worship with him and hear his songs of praise.
Or work with him in educating college students.
Or laugh with him at funny things
Enhanced by his wit.
Or cry with him when sorrow comes.
Or dine with him on food he lovingly prepared.

Or travel with him as citizens of God's world.
Or walk with him and talk along the way.
Or kneel with him and pray.

He is gone, Lord.
Death has claimed my love.

I stand at his grave and weep.
Are you here weeping with me, Lord?
Waiting to comfort me
When I reach out to You?

Please put your loving arms around me, Lord,
And hold me close.

OUTPOURINGS
OF COMFORT

"When Jesus therefore saw her weeping . . . he groaned in the spirit, and was troubled, and said, Where have ye laid him? They said unto him, Lord, come and see. Jesus wept." —*John 11:33–35*

"Jesus said unto her, I am the resurrection, and the life: he that believeth in me, though he were dead, yet shall he live." —*John 11:25*

"If in this life only we have hope in Christ, we are of all men most miserable. But now is Christ risen from the dead, and become the firstfruits of them that slept." —*1 Corinthians 15:19–20*

"So also is the resurrection of the dead. . . . It is sown a natural body, it is raised a spiritual body. There is a natural body, and there is a spiritual body." —*1 Corinthians 15:42, 44*

"And as we have borne the image of the earthy, we shall also bear the image of the heavenly." —*1 Corinthians 15:49*

"Behold, I show you a mystery; We shall not all sleep, but we shall all be changed, in a moment, in the twinkling of an eye, at the last trump: for the trumpet shall sound, and the dead shall be raised incorruptible, and we shall be changed. For this corruptible must put on incorruption, and this mortal must put on immortality. So when this corruptible shall have put on incorruption, and this mortal shall have put on immortality, then shall be brought to pass the saying that is written, Death is swallowed up in victory. O death, where is thy sting? O grave, where is thy victory? . . . But thanks be to God, which giveth us the victory through our Lord Jesus Christ."
—*1 Corinthians 15: 51–55, 57*

LISTENING FOR YOUR RETURN

OUTPOURINGS OF GRIEF

My heart listens for your return, my love.

I hear a plane overhead and think that you're
    flying home from Europe.
I hear a car turn into the driveway and believe
    that you're back!
I'm ready to rush to the door to welcome you
    and hear your glad words: "I'm home, darling!"
But you are not there.
I am the one to open the door each time
And say to an empty house, "I'm home, darling!"

In the store, I find myself still planning meals
    for both of us,
Or buying your favorite foods instead of mine.
And sometimes while I'm cooking dinner,
My heart hears you drive up outside.

It's only a daydream.
I must dine alone.

Perhaps if you had not been
Overseas when you died,
There would be no such fantasies.
My mind knows that you will not return to me.
My heart knows that I shall go to you.

I remember the time I flew alone to Amsterdam
To join you for the choir tour.
"What if he isn't there to meet me?
How will we make connections? I'm scared!"
I needn't have worried at all.
You were there, my love, waiting for me,
Waving your arms joyously,
And shouting, "Welcome, darling!"

You have gone ahead, my love.

And I shall join you there!
My heart anticipates your glad shout:

"Welcome, darling!"

OUTPOURINGS
OF COMFORT

"Then shall the dust return to the earth as it was:
and the spirit shall return unto God who gave it."
—*Ecclesiastes 12:7*

"As the cloud is consumed and vanisheth away; so
he that goeth down to the grave shall come up no
more. He shall return no more to his house, neither shall his place know him any more. Therefore
. . . I will speak in the anguish of my spirit; I will
complain in the bitterness of my soul."
—*Job 7:9–11*

"But now he [David's child] is dead, wherefore
should I fast? Can I bring him back again? I shall
go to him, but he shall not return to me."
—*2 Samuel 12:23*

"Sorrow not, even as others which have no hope. For if we believe that Jesus died and rose again, even so them also which sleep in Jesus will God bring with him. . . . Wherefore comfort one another with these words."
—*1 Thessalonians 4:13–14,18*

"Now is your time of grief, but I will see you again and you will rejoice, and no one will take away your joy." —*John 16:22 (NIV)*

My Outpourings

_____

_____

_____

_____

_____

_____

_____

WHY NOT NOW, LORD?

OUTPOURINGS OF GRIEF

In an instant, Lord,
You translated my beloved
From earth to heaven's bliss,
Leaving me a widow,
Bereaved and hurting,
To continue life alone.

I cannot bear this pain of separation.

Why not finish breaking my heart
This very moment, Lord,
And let me die, too?

We journeyed far together,
Serving You.
What joy 'twould be
To enter Heaven's gate

And meet him there!

Why not *now* for me too, Lord?

Your silence is Your answer?
I am to stay?
Still locked in earth's mortality?
Immortality must await
God's timing?

I trust your reasons, Lord,
Though I do not understand.
Please help me.

Outpourings
of Comfort

"Lover and friend hast thou put far from me."
—*Psalm 88:18*

"O that thou wouldest hide me in the grave."
—*Job 14:13*

"Casting down imaginations . . . and bringing into captivity every thought to the obedience of Christ." —*2 Corinthians 10:5*

"To everything there is a season, and a time to every purpose under the heaven: a time to be born, and a time to die." —*Ecclesiastes 3:1–2*

"Lord, make me to know mine end, and the measure of my days." —*Psalm 39:4*

"He [Jesus] answered her not a word."
—*Matthew 15:23*

"Wait on the Lord: be of good courage, and he shall strengthen thine heart: wait, I say, on the Lord." —*Psalm 27:14*

"'For I know the plans I have for you,' declares the LORD, 'plans to prosper you and not to harm you, plans to give you hope and a future.'"
—*Jeremiah 29:11 (NIV)*

"For I am in a strait betwixt two, having a desire to depart, and to be with Christ; which is far better: nevertheless to abide in the flesh is more needful for you." —*Philippians 1:23–24*

"My times are in thy hand." —*Psalm 31:15*

"Lord, I believe; help thou mine unbelief."
—*Mark 9:24*

WHO AM I, LORD?

OUTPOURINGS OF GRIEF

Who am I, Lord,
Now that my beloved is gone?

My earthly life was merged with his.
His work was my work, too.
Life partners—friends and lovers, too—
I was an extension of my beloved.
No longer is he here
To chart our course together.
I must journey on alone.

Who am I, Lord,
Now that my beloved is gone?

As my separate self,
Is there identity all my own?
His death has diminished me.

Loss has lessened my self-worth.
Tears blind my eyes,
And I cannot see
The special gift of self
That You have given me.

Who am I, Lord,
Now that my beloved is gone?

OUTPOURINGS
OF COMFORT

"I am like a pelican of the wilderness: I am like an owl of the desert. I watch, and am as a sparrow alone upon the house top." —*Psalm 102:6–7*

"I am like a broken vessel." —*Psalm 31:12*

"But by the grace of God I am what I am."
—*1 Corinthians 15:10*

"For ye are all the children of God by faith in Christ Jesus." —*Galatians 3:26*

"Having then gifts differing according to the grace that is given to us." —*Romans 12:6*

"But let every man prove his own work, and then shall he have rejoicing in himself alone, and not in another." —*Galatians 6:4*

"So then every one of us shall give account of himself to God." —*Romans 14:12*

My Outpourings

WHERE IS "HOME"?

OUTPOURINGS OF GRIEF

Where is "home," Lord,
Now that my beloved is gone?

We moved so often,
Doing Thy will,
Thy work for us at that time.
But soon each house became "home,"
For we were there *together*
With the children.

And then we'd move again!
It wasn't easy, Lord.
But soon that house
Became "home," too.
We were still *together*!

Now I am alone.

My beloved is gone.
The children, too,
Living their own lives,
As they should do.

This Florida house on Wilderness Road
Was to be our "home"
For sunset years together.

We were here so briefly—
Two working years.
There was no retirement then.
It is no longer "home."
It is just a house.
I cannot stay.

But where shall I go, Lord?
Where is "home"
Now that my beloved is gone?

OUTPOURINGS OF COMFORT

"In all thy ways acknowledge him, and he shall direct thy paths." —*Proverbs 3:6*

"Ye shall not go out with haste . . . for the LORD will go before you." —*Isaiah 52:12*

"Behold, I send an angel before thee, to keep thee in the way, and to bring thee into the place which I have prepared." —*Exodus 23:20*

"LORD, thou hast been our dwelling place in all generations." —*Psalm 90:1*

"Even unto this present hour we . . . have no certain dwelling place." —*1 Corinthians 4:11*

"I will instruct thee and teach thee in the way which thou shalt go: I will guide thee with mine eye." —*Psalm 32:8*

"For here have we no continuing city, but we seek one to come." —*Hebrews 13:14*

"Let not your heart be troubled. . . . In my Father's house are many mansions. . . . I go to prepare a place for you. And . . . I will come again, and receive you unto myself; that where I am, there ye may be also." —*John 14:1–3*

MY OUTPOURINGS

MY COMFORTERS

OUTPOURINGS OF GRIEF

I understand more about Job's comforters now,
  Lord,
For I have had comforters, too.

Family came.
We opened our arms to each other
And grieved at our loss,
Shared memories that would bless
And love that could help heal.

Friends came.
Some to weep with me,
Saying not a word
But surrounding me with love.
Some to embrace me in my grief
And tell me that they care.
Some to say, "I know exactly how you feel."

(How can they truly know?)
And some to preach to me,
Telling me to be brave and not cry,
To trust and not doubt.
Some comforters helped bear my burden.
Others added to it.
I know every comforter's intent was good, Father,
And I'm grateful for every one who cared enough
To come, to call, to write.

And then the Holy Spirit came,
The true Comforter whom You sent, Lord Jesus,
To anchor my life in Your love and truth
At this turbulent time
And to call to my remembrance Your words
That I need to hear.
The Holy Presence—
Calming my troubled spirit
And consoling my broken heart.

OUTPOURINGS
OF COMFORT

"Many Jews had come to Martha and Mary to comfort them in the loss of their brother."
—*John 11:19 (NIV)*

"Weep with them that weep." —*Romans 12:15*

"That their hearts might be comforted, being knit together in love." —*Colossians 2:2*

"May your unfailing love be my comfort."
—*Psalm 119:76 (NIV)*

"Blessed be God, even the Father of our Lord Jesus Christ, the Father of mercies, and the God of all comfort; who comforteth us in all our tribulation, that we may be able to comfort them which are in any trouble, by the comfort wherewith we ourselves are comforted of God." —*2 Corinthians 1:3–4*

"And I will pray the Father, and he shall give you another Comforter, that he may abide with you forever; even the Spirit of truth . . . I will not leave you comfortless: I will come to you."
—*John 14:16–18*

"Now our Lord Jesus Christ himself, and God, even our Father, which hath loved us, and hath given us everlasting consolation and good hope through grace, comfort your hearts."
—*2 Thessalonians 2:16–17*

MY OUTPOURINGS

EXPRESSIONS OF LOVE

OUTPOURINGS OF GRIEF

Thank You, Father, for all our friends
Who expressed their love in many ways.

By serving in our home—
Those special friends who helped for seven days,
Greeting guests,
Answering the phone,
Receiving flowers and caring for them,
Accepting food and serving it,
Entertaining my three-year-old granddaughter.

By giving gifts—
Of self
   by coming in person
   or by calling on the phone.
Of food
   to tempt my waning appetite,

and to feed family and friends staying here.
How comforting food can be at such times!
(I especially remember the key lime pie
a friend made.)
Of flowers
for the home
or for the cemetery.
Of contributions
to my husband's memorial fund
at the college.

By sending cards and letters—
Tributes to my beloved,
Sharing memories
Of how he had blessed their lives
And telling me how he had been their friend.
Comfort and encouragement for me,
Through their love and prayers,
Through their affirmation of my own self-worth

As I seek God's ongoing purpose for my life.
(Several of their messages have a special place
In my Comfort Box.)

By continuing to show their care—
Roses from a friend
Who waited 'til flowers ceased to come,
A phone call each Sunday for months
From my college roommate.
Calls from other faithful friends and family,
Visits from friends who brought food
Or took me out to eat.
Long trips the children made
To be with me and to help.

I'm deeply grateful, Father, for all these expressions of love.

OUTPOURINGS
OF COMFORT

"By love serve one another." —*Galatians 5:13*

"Bear ye one another's burdens, and so fulfil the law of Christ." —*Galatians 6:2*

"Nevertheless God, that comforteth those that are cast down, comforted us by the coming of Titus."
—*2 Corinthians 7:6*

"Let brotherly love continue." —*Hebrews 13:1*

"But to do good and to communicate forget not."
—*Hebrews 13:16*

"[God] who comforteth us in all our tribulation, that we may be able to comfort them which are in any trouble, by the comfort wherewith we ourselves are comforted of God." —*2 Corinthians 1:4*

"And Jonathan . . . went to David into the wood, and strengthened his hand in God."
—*1 Samuel 23:16*

"[Tychicus] whom I have sent unto you to comfort your hearts." —*Ephesians 6:22*

GRIEF'S INTENSITY

OUTPOURINGS OF GRIEF

Grief is *intense* tonight, Lord.

Pain racks my being,
Rends my heart,
Pierces my mind,
Disquiets my soul.

Can grief kill?
How long can I bear this agony?
Is there no balm in Gilead for broken hearts?

Your loving presence, Lord,
Is balm for those who grieve.
And underneath are the everlasting arms.
Gradually, grief's anguish
Will become sorrow's mourning,
And sorrow is a gentler companion than grief.

Meanwhile, Father,
Rock me in Your everlasting arms.
Let me rest in Your love.

OUTPOURINGS
OF COMFORT

"Have mercy upon me, O LORD . . . mine eye is consumed with grief." —*Psalm 31:9*

"Is there no balm in Gilead? is there no physician there? why then is not the health of the daughter of my people recovered?" —*Jeremiah 8:22*

"Let us therefore come boldly unto the throne of grace, that we may obtain mercy, and find grace to help in time of need." —*Hebrews 4:16*

"And he said unto me, My grace is sufficient for thee: for my strength is made perfect in weakness." —*2 Corinthians 12:9*

"He healeth the broken in heart, and bindeth up their wounds." —*Psalm 147:3*

"Why art thou cast down, O my soul? And why art thou disquieted within me? Hope thou in God: for I shall yet praise him, who is the health of my countenance, and my God." —*Psalm 42:11*

"The LORD hath heard the voice of my weeping. The LORD hath heard my supplication; the LORD will receive my prayer." —*Psalm 6:8–9*

"The eternal God is thy refuge, and underneath are the everlasting arms." —*Deuteronomy 33:27*

"He will quiet you with his love." —*Zephaniah 3:17 (NIV)*

My Outpourings

WHY AREN'T THEY MOURNING TOO?

OUTPOURINGS OF GRIEF

All around me are people living life as usual—
Working, shopping, laughing, eating,
Having fun, enjoying music, making plans.
Why aren't they mourning too?
Lord, I don't understand.

Don't they know that my beloved is dead?
Don't they know that life is devastated?
How can they be so uncaring?

At times I feel an impulse
To stop some happy stranger
And lash out at her,
"How can you be so full of life
When joy has gone from mine?
Why aren't you grieving with me?
Life is not the same!"

"And who are *you?*" she'd say.
"Your husband's death didn't touch *my world.*
My life is still happening
With work to do,
Relationships to enjoy,
And fun to have along the way.
I have a busy present and a bright future.
Do your own mourning."

Forgive me, Father.
Naively, I thought my husband's death
Had affected *everyone.*
There are some, of course, who mourn his passing,
But I am the one most profoundly hurt,
And I must do my *own* grieving.

I used to be one of the uncaring multitudes
Who hurried past those so burdened with sorrow.
My life went on as usual then.

But life will never be the same again for me.
I am now aware that others like myself,
Making their way unheeded through the crowds,
Are hurting too.
I am touched with compassion for them
And for the throngs
Who keep rushing past, living life as usual.
They, too, shall weep someday,
And then they'll understand.

OUTPOURINGS
OF COMFORT

"Is it nothing to you, all ye that pass by? Behold, and see if there be any sorrow like unto my sorrow." —*Lamentations 1:12*

"I am full of heaviness: and I looked for some to take pity, but there was none; and for comforters, but I found none." —*Psalm 69:20*

"Woe unto you that laugh now! for ye shall mourn and weep." —*Luke 6:25*

"But when he [Jesus] saw the multitudes, he was moved with compassion on them."
—*Matthew 9:36*

"Give therefore thy servant an understanding heart." —*1 Kings 3:9*

"Mourn with those who mourn."
—*Romans 12:15 (NIV)*

"Days should speak, and multitude of years should teach wisdom. But there is a spirit in man: and the inspiration of the Almighty giveth them understanding. Great men are not always wise: neither do the aged understand judgment." —*Job 32:7–9*

"But the wisdom that is from above is first pure, then peaceable, gentle, and easy to be entreated, full of mercy and good fruits, without partiality, and without hypocrisy." —*James 3:17*

SECTION TWO

DO YOU STILL
LOVE ME, DEAR?

DO YOU STILL LOVE ME, DEAR?

OUTPOURINGS OF GRIEF

Oh the sudden shock
Of knowing that you, my love,
Now see me as *I really am*.
Dying, your last words were,
"Tell Carolyn I love her."
But you were *mortal* then.

No longer earthly,
Your spirit is not blind
To all my faults and failings,
To my little hypocrisies and my sins.
There is no hiding anything from you.

I am ashamed.
How can you love me, dear,
Now that you know me as I really am?

But then I knew you, dear,
As far stronger than I.
Courageous in the face of death,
Always singing joyfully,
Uncomplaining about pain,
Believing all things possible with God.
So I was silent in my self,
Not confessing openly
My battles with limited faith.

You truly know me now, my love.
Do you love me still?

Yes, I know you do!
I feel your love affirming me,
Even as God's love does!
Why did it take so long to comprehend
That God has always seen me as I really am,
Yet loves me anyway?

OUTPOURINGS
OF COMFORT

"Many waters cannot quench love, neither can the floods drown it." —*Song of Solomon 8:7*

"Set me as a seal upon thine heart . . . for love is strong as death." —*Song of Solomon 8:6*

"I have loved thee with an everlasting love." —*Jeremiah 31:3*

"Love suffers long and is kind . . . bears all things, believes all things, hopes all things, endures all things. Love never fails." —*1 Corinthians 13:4, 7–8 (NKJV)*

"But God commendeth his love toward us, in that, while we were yet sinners, Christ died for us." —*Romans 5:8*

"Who shall separate us from the love of Christ? . . . For I am persuaded, that neither death, nor life . . . nor things present, nor things to come . . . shall be able to separate us from the love of God, which is in Christ Jesus our Lord." —*Romans 8:35, 38–39*

"O God, thou knowest my foolishness; and my sins are not hid from thee." —*Psalm 69:5*

My Outpourings

_____

_____

_____

_____

_____

_____

_____

_____

_____

_____

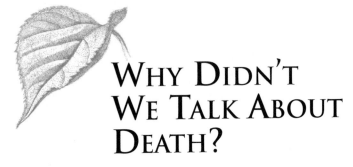

WHY DIDN'T WE TALK ABOUT DEATH?

OUTPOURINGS OF GRIEF

Why didn't we talk about death, my love?

There were many opportunities.
Surely death was standing near
When you had cancer,
A heart attack,
Brain surgery.
But all I heard you say
Was that God was *able*
And that you were not afraid to die.

Your optimism, your faith
That God would spare you yet again
Seemed to keep us from
Dwelling even for a moment
Upon death.

So I have no reservoir from which to draw
Shared thoughts and plans concerning death.
What comfort they would bring.

Why didn't we talk about death, my love?

I've had to make decisions
Relating to your death
Without the certainty
Of knowing your wishes.

Perhaps you simply trusted me
To do the best I could,
With God's help,
Whatever the circumstances of your death.

OUTPOURINGS OF COMFORT

"I will speak in the anguish of my spirit."
—*Job 7:11*

"If a man die, shall he live again?" —*Job 14:14*

"The living know that they shall die."
—*Ecclesiastes 9:5*

"I perceive that there is nothing better, than that a man should rejoice in his own works; for that is his portion." —*Ecclesiastes 3:22*

"To every thing there is a season, and a time to every purpose under the heaven." —*Ecclesiastes 3:1*

"For to me to live is Christ, and to die is gain."
—*Philippians 1:21*

"The heart of her husband doth safely trust in her."
—*Proverbs 31:11*

My Outpourings

WHY SUCH GUILT, LORD?

OUTPOURINGS OF GRIEF

Why didn't I . . . ?

Oh, the self-recrimination, God,
Now that my beloved is dead.

Why didn't I
Make him slow down
And take time for rest?

Why didn't I
Make him lose weight
And exercise more?

Why didn't I
Insist that he not take
That short business trip abroad?
Foolishly, I thought it would help

To distance himself briefly
From the stress of his college presidency.

Why didn't I
Go *with him* overseas
Instead of waiting for the second trip
A few months later
As we had planned?

At times my load of guilt is too heavy to bear.

But, Lord, why didn't *he*
Slow down and rest and live?

Why didn't *he*
Make time to see a doctor?
Headlong, he rushed into the future
With his dreams,
Ignoring present warnings from a worn-out body.

He made those choices;
They were his own choosing.

I do not have to bear the total guilt.
We are equally to blame.

OUTPOURINGS OF COMFORT

"My guilt has overwhelmed me like a burden too heavy to bear." —*Psalm 38:4 (NIV)*

"And ye shall know the truth, and the truth shall make you free." —*John 8:32*

"Casting all your care upon him; for he careth for you." —*1 Peter 5:7*

"For he knoweth our frame; he remembereth that we are dust." —*Psalm 103:14*

"But there is forgiveness with thee." —*Psalm 130:4*

"But unto you that fear my name shall the Sun of righteousness arise with healing in his wings." —*Malachi 4:2*

"Let us lay aside every weight, and the sin which doth so easily beset us, and let us run with patience the race that is set before us, looking unto Jesus the author and finisher of our faith."
—*Hebrews 12:1–2*

"And the peace of God, which passeth all understanding, shall keep your hearts and minds through Christ Jesus." —*Philippians 4:7*

MY OUTPOURINGS

_____

_____

_____

_____

_____

_____

_____

WEEPING

OUTPOURINGS OF GRIEF

Lord, when will my weeping stop?

The sudden shock of losing him
Shut out my tears at first,
Enabling me to handle necessary tasks
Of telling family and friends,
Making funeral arrangements,
Attending services.

Now, torrents of tears flow unbidden
Each time I wake from sleep and face again
The reality of death.

And unexpected provocations trigger tears—
Seeing a caring friend,
Reading a word of comfort,
Hearing a favorite hymn,

Seeing his clothes still hanging there,
Touching some object that unlocks a memory.

I am vulnerable and cannot stem the tears.

Surely You understand, Lord,
For You wept at Lazarus' tomb.
Please enfold me in Your loving arms
And weep with me.

Then, in the fullness of Your time, Lord,
Let this weeping pass.

OUTPOURINGS
OF COMFORT

"The LORD hath heard the voice of my weeping.
The LORD hath heard my supplication; the LORD
will receive my prayer." —*Psalm 6:8–9*

"When Jesus therefore saw her [Mary] weeping,
and the Jews also weeping which came with her,
he groaned in the spirit, and was troubled, and
said, Where have ye laid him [Lazarus]? They said
unto him, Lord, come and see. Jesus wept."
—*John 11:33–35*

"Mine eye poureth out tears unto God."
—*Job 16:20*

"Put thou my tears into thy bottle: are they not in
thy book?" —*Psalm 56:8*

"Hear my prayer, O LORD, and give ear unto my
cry; hold not thy peace at my tears."
—*Psalm 39:12*

"To everything there is a season . . . a time to
weep." —*Ecclesiastes 3:1, 4*

"And God shall wipe away all tears from their eyes." —*Revelation 7:17*

"For thou hast delivered my soul from death, mine eyes from tears, and my feet from falling."
—*Psalm 116:8*

MY OUTPOURINGS

_____

_____

_____

_____

_____

_____

_____

_____

SLEEP

OUTPOURINGS OF GRIEF

Sleep eludes me, Lord!
I need it so.

My body is exhausted.
My mind is weary, too.
But when I close my eyes to sleep,
Thoughts crowd my mind,
Pushing sleep away.

Or if I finally doze,
I waken soon, as though programmed
Only for catnaps,
And must wrestle with reality
Instead of dreams.

Oftimes, I simply rise and work.
One o'clock, two o'clock, three . . .

Sorting through boxes of memories
With sleep-hungry eyes.

Sometimes I claim Your promise
Of giving songs in the night.
I switch on the light,
Turn the pages of the hymnal I keep nearby,
And let music comfort me
As I hear it in my mind.

At other times I lie still
And rest upon Your promises,
Inserting my name in each one.

Often I reach out to touch my beloved.
He isn't there!
Startled, I wake to face once more
The fact of his death.

Lord Jesus, will I ever sleep peacefully again?

This, too, shall pass, You say?
In time, sleep will befriend me
And bring rest and renewal?
Meanwhile, I must rest in Thee.

OUTPOURINGS OF COMFORT

"By night on my bed I sought him whom my soul
loveth: I sought him, but I found him not."
—*Song of Solomon 3:1*

"Wearisome nights are appointed to me. When I
lie down, I say, When shall I arise, and the night
be gone? And I am full of tossings to and fro unto
the dawning of the day." —*Job 7:3–4*

"Return unto thy rest, O my soul." —*Psalm 116:7*

"Come unto me, all ye that labor and are heavy
laden, and I will give you rest." —*Matthew 11:28*

"Where is God my maker, who giveth songs in the
night?" —*Job 35:10*

"My eyes stay open through the watches of the night, that I may meditate on your promises."
—*Psalm 119:148 (NIV)*

"Whereby are given unto us exceeding great and precious promises." —*2 Peter 1:4*

"Rest in the LORD, and wait patiently for him."
—*Psalm 37:7*

"Thou shalt lie down, and thy sleep shall be sweet." —*Proverbs 3:24*

"I laid me down and slept; I awaked; for the LORD sustained me." —*Psalm 3:5*

DEPRESSED

OUTPOURINGS OF GRIEF

Yes, Lord, I know that I'm depressed.
I've no desire to live.
After all, my reason for living is gone.
I want to be with my beloved.

My body is fatigued.
Why shouldn't it be?
I cannot sleep at night.
Food repels; I am weak from losing thirty pounds.
Arthritis has flared up again,
Making it painful to walk.
Bed seems the best place to stay.

My mind is weary, too.
Tired of dealing with problems
And of making so many decisions.
Exhausted from remembering my beloved is gone

And isn't here to cheer and help.
Sadness accompanies me wherever I go.
There is no joy in living.

You say I must get up and get busy helping others?

My ninety-three-year-old mother-in-law
Needs more of my attention?
She is hurting deeply, too?

Our daughter's wedding is drawing near,
And I must help make it a joyful occasion?

And there is a job opportunity
To teach temporarily at the college?
To use my mind and my gifts?
Staying busy helping others will also help *me*, Lord?

Please take my hand. I want to rise and walk.

OUTPOURINGS
OF COMFORT

"I am a burden to myself." —*Job 7:20*

"My heart is smitten, and withered like grass; so that I forget to eat my bread." —*Psalm 102:4*

"Have mercy upon me, O LORD; for I am weak: O LORD, heal me; for my bones are vexed." —*Psalm 6:2*

"I am troubled; I am bowed down greatly; I go mourning all the day long." —*Psalm 38:6*

"Withhold not thou thy tender mercies from me, O LORD." —*Psalm 40:11*

"The sacrifices of God are a broken spirit: a broken and contrite heart, O God, thou wilt not despise." —*Psalm 51:17*

"Cast thy burden upon the LORD, and he shall sustain thee." —*Psalm 55:22*

"And the angel of the LORD came again the second time, and touched him, and said, Arise and eat; because the journey is too great for thee."
—*1 Kings 19:7*

"Why art thou cast down, O my soul? And why art thou disquieted within me? Hope thou in God: for I shall yet praise him, who is the health of my countenance, and my God." —*Psalm 42:11*

"We are troubled on every side, yet not distressed; we are perplexed, but not in despair . . . cast down but not destroyed." —*2 Corinthians 4:8–9*

"Be of good comfort, rise . . . He calleth thee."
—*Mark 10:49*

"He brought me up also out of a horrible pit, out of the miry clay, and set my feet upon a rock, and established my goings." —*Psalm 40:2*

WHY, FATHER? WHY?

OUTPOURINGS OF GRIEF

Why, Father? Why?
Why did you take my beloved from me?

Was it to punish me
With loneliness and grief
For sins I have committed?
Losing him was life's *greatest* loss.

How could You hurt me so cruelly?

If his death were truly Your way of chastening me,
Then You are only to be *feared*, Father,
Not loved and trusted.

I have loved and trusted You
These many years,
And my heart tells me

His death was not Your means
Of punishing me.
So I shall love and trust You still.

But why, Father? Why?
I do not understand.

Neither did my beloved.
Dying, he said,
"The Father wants me.
I don't understand.
There's so much more to do.
Tell Carolyn I love her."
And he died, serenely trusting You in death
Even as he had trusted You in life.

Was his earthly future bleak
With pain and helplessness?
Was death his highest good?

Was his work for You completed?
Did You, in *love*, call him home?

Your reasons are shrouded in mystery, Father.
But I trust You still.
Someday I'll understand.

OUTPOURINGS
OF COMFORT

"And as Jesus passed by, he saw a man which was
blind from his birth. And his disciples asked him,
saying, Master, who did sin, this man, or his parents, that he was born blind? Jesus answered,
Neither hath this man sinned, nor his parents: but
that the works of God should be made manifest in
him." —*John 9:1–3*

"Precious in the sight of the LORD is the death of
his saints." —*Psalm 116:15*

"Our heart is not turned back . . . though thou
hast sore broken us . . . and covered us with the
shadow of death." —*Psalm 44:18–19*

"Though he slay me, yet will I trust in him."
—*Job 13:15*

"The righteous perish . . . devout men are taken away, and no one understands that the righteous are taken away to be spared from evil."
—*Isaiah 57:1 (NIV)*

"Man's days are determined; you have decreed the number of his months and have set limits he cannot exceed." —*Job 14:5 (NIV)*

"For now we see through a glass, darkly, but then face to face: now I know in part; but then shall I know even as also I am known." —*1 Corinthians 13:12*

"For thou art my hope, O LORD God: thou art my trust from my youth." —*Psalm 71:5*

I'M ANGRY, FATHER!

OUTPOURINGS OF GRIEF

I'm angry, Father!
Angry with *You* for taking
My beloved from me,
Angry with *life* for
Crippling me so,
Angry with *my beloved* for
Dying and leaving me,
Angry with *myself* for
Being angry!

I'm angry
That my dear husband isn't here to help me.
(I was always there to help him.)
Angry that he didn't take better care of himself.
Angry that he didn't see a doctor sooner.
Angry that he didn't slow down and have us
Do the things we'd planned together.

Lord, how can I possibly be angry with my beloved?

Death was not his choosing.
He loved me and wanted to live.
He was just too busy doing Your work, Father,
And loved doing it!
Always, he put others' needs before his own.
Neglecting himself
But never neglecting others.
He trusted Your will in all things.

So why should I lash out at You, Father,
When I know Your will is truly best
And that his love for me
Was a special gift from You?

Is anger a natural part of grief?
Must it be acknowledged and expressed
Before healing can come?

Let anger dissipate, Lord,
And Your peace flow in to take its place.

OUTPOURINGS OF COMFORT

"Be ye angry, and sin not: let not the sun go down upon your wrath." —*Ephesians 4:26*

"Let all bitterness, and wrath, and anger . . . be put away from you." —*Ephesians 4:31*

"Cease from anger, and forsake wrath."
—*Psalm 37:8*

"And the Lord direct your hearts into the love of God." —*2 Thessalonians 3:5*

"Peace be with you all that are in Christ Jesus."
—*1 Peter 5:14*

"And the peace of God, which passeth all understanding, shall keep your hearts and minds through Christ Jesus." —*Philippians 4:7*

"Peace I [Jesus] leave with you, my peace I give unto you: not as the world giveth, give I unto you. Let not your heart be troubled, neither let it be afraid." —*John 14:27*

My Outpourings

_____

_____

_____

_____

_____

_____

_____

_____

_____

_____

SPECIAL DAYS
ARE HARDER

OUTPOURINGS
OF GRIEF

Today is our fortieth wedding anniversary, dear.
My first without you.
Pain pierces my heart.
I miss you so.

Special days are harder than ordinary ones.

More than a year has passed since your death.
I've hurt through many special days.
First there was your birthday,
Then Thanksgiving,
And Christmas,
Valentine's Day,
And Easter,
My birthday,
And now our wedding anniversary.
Ordinary days are hard enough to bear;

Special days are almost unbearable.

Each special day brings special memories
Of times we spent together.
Those memories further rend my broken heart.
Will it always be like this, Father?

The first year is the hardest
In the calendar of recovery.
Time will diminish the intensity of my grief.
And those special-day memories will become
Very special blessings in my life.

Hurry time along, I pray.

Outpourings of Comfort

"In quietness and in confidence shall be your strength." —*Isaiah 30:15*

"I will go in the strength of the LORD God." —*Psalm 71:16*

"God is our refuge and strength, a very present help in trouble." —*Psalm 46:1*

"Wait on the LORD: be of good courage, and he shall strengthen thine heart: wait, I say, on the LORD." —*Psalm 27:14*

"But the God of all grace, who hath called us unto his eternal glory by Christ Jesus, after that ye have suffered a while, make you perfect, stablish, strengthen, settle you." —*1 Peter 5:10*

"Weeping may endure for a night, but joy cometh in the morning." —*Psalm 30:5*

My Outpourings

HURRICANE!

OUTPOURINGS OF GRIEF

Hurricane Andrew bypassed West Palm Beach
And devastated Homestead!
Forecasters were uncertain just where it would hit.

I waited for it during that long, dark night
With a widow friend and her two grandchildren.
She had invited me to stay with her,
For her house has storm shutters.
Mine has no protection.

Friends helped move outdoor furniture inside,
And I had stocked up on water and other supplies.
I did the best I could without you, dear,
But I *needed* you.

God brought me safely through that hurricane.
How many still lie ahead of me?

Not just South Florida hurricanes,
But fierce storms of life
To batter me while I'm alone.

But I'm *not* alone, Lord.
You are with me always,
And I need not fear the storms.

Please help me trust You so completely
That I shall not be afraid.

OUTPOURINGS
OF COMFORT

"Fearfulness and trembling are come upon me. . . .
Oh that I had wings like a dove! For then would I
fly away, and be at rest. . . . I would hasten my
escape from the windy storm and tempest."
—*Psalm 55:5–6, 8*

"For he shall give his angels charge over thee, to
keep thee in all thy ways." —*Psalm 91:11*

"Then they cry unto the LORD in their trouble,
and he bringeth them out of their distresses. He
maketh the storm a calm, so that the waves
thereof are still. Then are they glad because they
be quiet; so he bringeth them unto their desired
haven." —*Psalm 107:28–30*

"And there arose a great storm of wind, and the
waves beat into the ship, so that it was now full.
And he [Jesus] was in the hinder part of the ship,
asleep on a pillow: and they [the disciples] awake
him, and say unto him, Master, carest thou not
that we perish? And he arose, and rebuked the
wind, and said unto the sea, Peace, be still. And
the wind ceased, and there was a great calm. And

he said unto them, Why are ye so fearful? how is it that ye have no faith?" —*Mark 4:37–40*

"Lo, I am with you alway, even unto the end of the world." —*Matthew 28:20*

"I will trust, and not be afraid: for the LORD JEHOVAH is my strength and my song." —*Isaiah 12:2*

MY OUTPOURINGS

_____

_____

_____

_____

_____

_____

FORGIVENESS

OUTPOURINGS OF GRIEF

While there in Paris, dear,
On the day of your death,
You stopped at Notre Dame Cathedral
And prayed for one who had wronged you greatly,
Forgiving him and asking God to bless his life.

You left with lighter step,
With peace and joy,
To continue your journey to the airport—
And to death.

Forgiving and forgiven,
You stepped out into eternity,
At peace with God,
With your fellowman,
And with yourself.

Father, teach me Your lesson of forgiveness.
Call to my remembrance whomever You wish.
And as the memories stream past,
Help me pause wherever forgiveness is needed.
As Your divine love shines full
Upon me and my adversary,
Help me release all anger and bitterness.
Only then can Your healing love
Restore and bless us both.

Forgive and I shall be forgiven.
What an eternal lesson, Lord!
I confess my own sins, Father,
And ask Thy forgiveness,
Knowing that in Your love and mercy,
You are ready to forgive me, too.

I must also forgive *myself*, Father?
But that is hard to do! Please help me.

Outpourings
of Comfort

"And forgive us our debts, as we forgive our debtors." —*Matthew 6:12*

"For if ye forgive men their trespasses, your heavenly Father will also forgive you: but if ye forgive not men their trespasses, neither will your Father forgive your trespasses." —*Matthew 6:14–15*

"And be ye kind one to another, tenderhearted, forgiving one another, even as God for Christ's sake hath forgiven you." —*Ephesians 4:32*

"Forbearing one another, and forgiving one another, if any man have a quarrel against any: even as Christ forgave you, so also do ye." —*Colossians 3:13*

"If we confess our sins, he is faithful and just to forgive us our sins, and to cleanse us from all unrighteousness." —*1 John 1:9*

"Have mercy upon me, O God, according to thy loving-kindness: according unto the multitude of thy tender mercies blot out my transgressions. . . .

For I acknowledge my transgressions: and my sin is ever before me." —*Psalm 51:1, 3*

"Her sins, which are many, are forgiven; for she loved much: but to whom little is forgiven, the same loveth little. And he [Jesus] said unto her, Thy sins are forgiven. . . . go in peace."
—*Luke 7: 47–48, 50*

"Create in me a clean heart, O God; and renew a right spirit within me." —*Psalm 51:10*

MY OUTPOURINGS

MY UNWAVERING MIDDLE C

OUTPOURINGS OF GRIEF

My dear,
You said I was your "unwavering middle C."

You were all the music of my life—
Bringing spontaneity,
Laughter, joy, love,
Strength, tenderness, worship, rapture.

Through romantic love songs,
Merry childhood melodies,
Thundering operas,
Magnificent concertos,
Scintillating symphonies,
Heartwarming gospel songs,
Worshipful hymns,
Majestic oratorios,
Glorious anthems.

Father, You took the music from my life,
Leaving me bereft.
Unaccompanied.

I cannot bear to hear
Music that we shared.
It touches me at depths beyond control
And shakes my inner being.

How can I sing the Lord's song
In this strange land of grief?

Bring back the music to my life, Lord.
Creator of music, please gift my life
With heart-healing music
That comforts, strengthens, and sustains.

Perhaps some day
I shall again sing praises to Thy Name.

OUTPOURINGS OF COMFORT

"My harp is tuned to mourning, and my flute to the sound of wailing." —*Job 30:31 (NIV)*

"How shall we sing the Lord's song in a strange land?" —*Psalm 137:4*

"Sing unto the LORD a new song, and his praise from the end of the earth." —*Isaiah 42:10*

"Speaking to yourselves in psalms and hymns and spiritual songs, singing and making melody in your heart to the Lord." —*Ephesians 5:19*

"And he hath put a new song in my mouth, even praise unto our God: many shall see it, and fear, and shall trust in the LORD." —*Psalm 40:3*

My Outpourings

LOVING LAUGHTER

OUTPOURINGS OF GRIEF

Will I ever laugh again now that you are gone, my love?

Your keen sense of humor leavened our life together. I remember the *Harmony Pot* and the *Trouble Book*. Through them you injected healthy, healing laughter into our marital quarrels.

Whenever we argued about something, and disharmony reigned, you would ceremoniously lift out the Harmony Pot (a small flower pot) from its brass musical staff mounted on the wall.

Then you would proceed to make an official entry in our family Trouble Book. Finally, you would present the document for me to cosign. After reading aloud your hilarious account of our disagreement, we were able to laugh about it, and harmony was restored.

Likewise, your warm wit leavened your ministry of serving God. Facing a large and noisy audience of boys at the Brazilian Royal Ambassador Congress in Rio de Janeiro, Brazil, you asked a missionary on stage with you the Portuguese word for "quiet." Then you secured a seemingly miraculous hush by dramatically singing in a commanding and prolonged tone, "Silencio!"

You had won over your rowdy audience through your quick wit in giving an impromptu "operatic" performance in their own language!

Heavenly Father, please use the funny, happy memories of Claude's loving laughter to help heal my grief.

OUTPOURINGS
OF COMFORT

"A merry heart maketh a cheerful countenance:
but by sorrow of the heart the spirit is broken."
—*Proverbs 15:13*

"A merry heart doeth good like a medicine: but a
broken spirit drieth up the bones."
—*Proverbs 17:22*

"A time to weep, and a time to laugh; a time to
mourn, and a time to dance." —*Ecclesiastes 3:4*

"Then was our mouth filled with laughter, and our
tongue with singing." —*Psalm 126:2*

"Thou hast put gladness in my heart." —*Psalm 4:7*

"Blessed are ye that weep now: for ye shall laugh."
—*Luke 6:21*

My Outpourings

PEACE AND TENDER MEMORIES

OUTPOURINGS OF GRIEF

In kindness
A friend wished me
"Peace and tender memories."

I have no abiding peace yet, Lord,
About my beloved's death.
My heart is crushed.
In my bereavement I cry out to You in pain.

And memories of our times together
Are "tender" indeed—
So tender that even touching them
Cuts too sharply to bear.

Surely they will become
Tender loving memories
That heal and bless.

But *when*, Lord?

When will the memories *bless*?

And when will I find Thy peace?

OUTPOURINGS OF COMFORT

"Hath God forgotten to be gracious? Hath he in anger shut up his tender mercies?" —*Psalm 77:9*

"And thou hast removed my soul far off from peace. . . . remembering mine affliction and my misery. . . . My soul hath them still in remembrance." —*Lamentations 3:17,19–20*

"For he is our peace." —*Ephesians 2:14*

"These things have I spoken unto you, that in me ye might have peace. In the world ye shall have tribulation: but be of good cheer; I have overcome the world." —*John 16:33*

"And the peace of God, which passeth all understanding, shall keep your hearts and minds through Christ Jesus." —*Philippians 4:7*

"But the fruit of the Spirit is . . . peace." —*Galatians 5:22*

"Whatsoever things are lovely . . . think on these things." —*Philippians 4:8*

MY OUTPOURINGS

_____

_____

_____

_____

_____

_____

_____

_____

_____

_____

_____

_____

_____

_____

_____

_____

_____

_____

_____

_____

_____

_____

_____

PRIVATE PAIN, PUBLIC SUNSHINE

OUTPOURINGS OF GRIEF

Garbed in *mourning*—
Tears, sadness, loneliness, self-pity—
I relate to others
At church,
In my neighborhood,
In the marketplace.

"How are you?" Some stop to ask.

Do they *really* want to know?
Shall I reply, "I'm hurting so . . . "
And rain my woes on them?

Or shall I continue as before and say,
"I'm hanging in with God's help.
Thank you for asking."
Then quietly move on?

My grief is *private* pain, Father.
I must mourn alone with Thee
in my own secluded Garden of Gethsemane.

Grief is not for public display
As I wander alone among the busy multitudes.
I want to walk in *public sunshine*,
Not in *clouds of grief*.

Let Thy Son shine through me, Father;
And when someone asks, "How are you?"
Help me gently smile and say,
"All is well because of Jesus."

Private pain, Lord—*alone* with Thee;
Public sunshine with *others*—through God's grace.

OUTPOURINGS
OF COMFORT

"I am troubled; I am bowed down greatly; I go mourning all the day long." —*Psalm 38:6*

"Blessed are they that mourn: for they shall be comforted." —*Matthew 5:4*

"But thou, when thou prayest, enter into thy closet, and when thou hast shut thy door, pray to thy Father which is in secret; and thy Father which seeth in secret shall reward thee openly." —*Matthew 6:6*

"And when he [Jesus] had sent the multitudes away, he went up into a mountain apart to pray." —*Matthew 14:23*

"Then cometh Jesus with them unto a place called Gethsemane, and saith unto the disciples, Sit ye here, while I go and pray yonder." —*Matthew 26:36*

"Looking unto Jesus the author and finisher of our faith." —*Hebrews 12:2*

"Now when they saw the boldness of Peter and John, and perceived that they were unlearned and ignorant men, they marveled; and they took knowledge of them, that they had been with Jesus." —*Acts 4:13*

"Truly our fellowship is with the Father, and with his Son Jesus Christ. . . . God is light, and in him is no darkness at all. . . . if we walk in the light, as he is in the light, we have fellowship one with another." —*1 John 1:3, 5, 7*

"In thy light shall we see light." —*Psalm 36:9*

"The LORD make his face shine upon thee . . . and give thee peace." —*Numbers 6:25–26*

FAMILY

OUTPOURINGS OF GRIEF

Our children, dear, are a special gift from God.
They blessed our mortal life together
And continue to bless mine.

They came quickly upon learning of your death
And helped in many ways.
We wept together at losing you
But rejoiced to have had the blessing of your presence
Those years together.
Our older son spoke for us as a family
At your funeral service.

We came together again for Meg's wedding
Five months after your death.
You helped plan it, and she kept it just that way.
So, as family, we created a happy memory
To treasure through the years.

The children came again to join me in Missouri
For your mother's funeral
Almost seventeen months after your own.
All three spoke briefly at her service,
Sharing memories and love
Beautifully!

We cannot get together as often as we used to do,
But we are close in many ways,
And grandchildren are binding us even closer.
Elizabeth is the only grandchild who knew you.
She remembers your love and laughter,
Your fun and music,
And can pass those memories on.
She still sings the children's songs we wrote!
Our other grandchildren will sing them, too.

Claude and Carolyn have another daughter now,
Little Mary.

Meg and Dave have their Melissa and Katie.
Randy and Elaine await God's will and time
Concerning a child for them.

We are still family, dear,
Though you are gone from sight.
Your spirit binds us close together
And enriches all our lives.

OUTPOURINGS OF COMFORT

"God setteth the solitary in families." —*Psalm* 68:6

"Lo, children are a heritage of the LORD: and the fruit of the womb is his reward." —*Psalm 127:3*

"Thy wife shall be as a fruitful vine by the sides of thine house: thy children like olive plants round about thy table." —*Psalm 128:3*

"And all thy children shall be taught of the LORD; and great shall be the peace of thy children."
—*Isaiah 54:13*

"A son honoreth his father." —*Malachi 1:6*

"Above all, love each other deeply, because love covers over a multitude of sins."
—*1 Peter 4:8 (NIV)*

"Let us consider how we may spur one another on toward love and good deeds."
—*Hebrews 10:24 (NIV)*

"Now also when I am old and grayheaded, O God, forsake me not; until I have showed thy strength unto this generation, and thy power to everyone that is to come." —*Psalm 71:18*

"I have no greater joy than to hear that my children walk in truth." —*3 John 4*

I Am Loved!

OUTPOURINGS OF GRIEF

I am loved!
Your final words, my dear, were these:
"Tell Carolyn I love her."
What a priceless gift to treasure in my heart!
Somehow you knew I needed that remembrance.

Yes, I am loved
By *you*, my *special one*,
With whom I shared my life.

I am loved
By *family* and *friends*,
Who hurt with me and care.

I am loved
By my *Heavenly Father*,
Who so loved the world

(And I am one of those He so loved!)
That He gave His only begotten Son
To be our Savior.

I am loved
By my Savior, Jesus Christ,
Who lived and died in human form
To be the Way, the Truth, and the Life.

I am loved
By *me*.
"Love your neighbor as yourself," Christ said.
Lord, help me love myself in wholesome ways
That keep me growing in Your will.
Then, in turn, please help me
Love my neighbor as myself.

Yes, I am loved
With an everlasting love!

Heart-healing love!
Soul-strengthening love!
Joy-filled love!

Father, help me communicate Your love to others.

OUTPOURINGS
OF COMFORT

"Husbands, love your wives, even as Christ also
loved the church, and gave himself for it."
—*Ephesians 5:25*

"The heart of her husband doth safely trust in
her." —*Proverbs 31:11*

"A friend loveth at all times." —*Proverbs 17:17*

"For God so loved the world, that he gave his only
begotten Son, that whosoever believeth in him
should not perish, but have everlasting life."
—*John 3:16*

"I have loved thee with an everlasting love."
—*Jeremiah 31:3*

"He that hath my commandments, and keepeth them, he it is that loveth me: and he that loveth me shall be loved of my Father, and I will love him, and will manifest myself to him."
—*John 14:21*

"Who shall separate us from the love of Christ?"
—*Romans 8:35*

"Thou shalt love thy neighbor as thyself."
—*Galatians 5:14*

"And this I pray, that your love may abound yet more and more in knowledge and in all judgment."
—*Philippians 1:9*

MY SEPARATE SELF

OUTPOURINGS OF GRIEF

Who am I, God,
Now that I'm only *me*?

Humbly, I stand in Thy presence
As my separate self—
Alone with Thee.

Am I still Thy child,
Father, though really an *adult*?
Please speak to my broken heart.

You are My beloved daughter—
Conceived in My mind,
Created in My image,
Imbued with boundless potential,
Endowed with special gifts
To equip you for life's journey.

But, Father, I am so weak.
How can I possibly become
The wonderful person
You envision me to be?

My child, Christ will show you the way.
He is My eternal truth,
The everlasting expression of My love.
Already, He is your Savior.
Let Him be your teacher
And your friend.

I do trust Him, Father!

With Christ's presence guiding me,
And Thy love through Him affirming me,
Help me grow toward becoming on Earth
The person You will complete in Heaven.

OUTPOURINGS OF COMFORT

"For ye are all the children of God by faith in Christ Jesus." —*Galatians 3:26*

"Neglect not the gift that is in thee." —*1 Timothy 4:14*

"But by the grace of God I am what I am." —*1 Corinthians 15:10*

"For we are his workmanship, created in Christ Jesus unto good works, which God hath before ordained that we should walk in them." —*Ephesians 2:10*

"Know ye not your own selves, how that Jesus Christ is in you?" —*2 Corinthians 13:5*

"Glorify God in your body, and in your spirit, which are God's." —*1 Corinthians 6:20*

"Study to show thyself approved unto God, a workman that needeth not to be ashamed, rightly dividing the word of truth." —*2 Timothy 2:15*

"May the God of peace . . . equip you with everything good for doing his will, and may he work in us what is pleasing to him, through Jesus Christ, to whom be glory for ever and ever. Amen."
—*Hebrews 13:20–21 (NIV)*

My Outpourings

_____

_____

_____

_____

_____

_____

_____

_____

_____

SORTING THROUGH THE PAST

OUTPOURINGS OF GRIEF

At last, your clothes are gone, my dear.
I've given them away.
For a long while, I couldn't part with them
And kept them in your closet as they always were.
You no longer need them.
You're clothed in immortality.

I've made a start toward
Sorting through your life and your belongings.
You collected souvenirs of all kinds
While traveling around the world.
You were quite a collector!
Before I can move to a smaller place,
I must let go of things
We thought would wait for many years.
I want the children to decide
What they wish to keep.

We did the same with your mother's things
Stored in Missouri, dear.
I wanted only your boxes of letters and memorabilia.
The children divided the rest.

Oh, the boxes, dear!
I added the Missouri memories
To the eighty-five boxes
Brought to me from the college.
You always had them shipped ahead
To your next job,
Not mingling them with family items.
You planned to look through them
During retirement
And to enjoy the memories.
Now the task is mine.

Boxes of correspondence,
Clippings, pictures, speeches, articles,

Books, music, programs, plans, dreams,
Diplomas, honors, awards.
Your life—reduced to paper.
But oh, what treasures they hold.
It's like putting together
The jigsaw puzzle of your life.
    Your childhood,
    Your high school years,
    Your army years (books and letters such as those
    about the war crimes trials in Nuremberg while
    you were stationed there),
    Your college years (our love letters to each other!)
    Your work and ministry through the years.
I know you even better now, my love.

Father, please help me
Sort through the clutter of Claude's life and mine,
Keeping only precious treasures,
And gently leaving the rest behind.

OUTPOURINGS
OF COMFORT

"I thought about the former days, the years of long
ago." —*Psalm 77:5 (NIV)*

"From a child thou hast known the holy Scriptures, which are able to make thee wise unto salvation through faith which is in Christ Jesus."
—*2 Timothy 3:15*

"The LORD is my strength and my shield; my heart trusted in him, and I am helped: therefore my heart greatly rejoiceth; and with my song will I praise him." —*Psalm 28:7*

"The steps of a good man are ordered by the LORD: and he delighteth in his way." —*Psalm 37:23*

"I will make thee . . . a joy of many generations."
—*Isaiah 60:15*

"I have fought a good fight, I have finished my course, I have kept the faith." —*2 Timothy 4:7*

LOVE LETTERS

OUTPOURINGS OF GRIEF

Darling, what treasures I'm finding in some of the boxes I'm going through: letters I wrote you and letters and notes you wrote me! Often, when you were going away, you'd leave a note on my pillow.

Several of your letters opened with these lines from our favorite love poem:

*"I love you not only for what you are but for what I am when I'm with you."**

After the bus in which you were riding back to college was in an accident, you wrote:

"It's strange how, as I thought the end of my life was near, I sent my thoughts of love winging to you. I love you not only in this life but in that one to come."

During a crisis time in my life, you penned these

words to me:

"Three certainties, my love—even during the flood times of life: One, God is able. Two, God knows your name and cares. Three, God loves you and so do I! Be at peace, then. Rest upon His timing. This too shall pass."

You shared these thoughts when we were seeking God's will for your life-ministry:

"You know, sweetheart, I've been thinking a lot lately about what real success is. I used to believe it would be in some important post—but my concept of success has changed. True success is serving God to the best of your capacity in the place where He wants you to be."

And from Santiago, Chile, you sent me the gift of this treasured message:

"Darling, the drive to serve God has sometimes

caused me to seem unthoughtful. For this I ask your forgiveness and understanding. You have given me the opportunity and freedom to put Christ as pre-eminent. In so doing, our love has more dimension. Please accept my heart and my love—even across these long miles that separate us today."

In one of your notes, you greeted me this way:
   "Good morning, love. It's a beautiful day! May you know bottom-line that God is on His throne and all is right. Hang in there today, and always know I love you eternally!"

Thank you, darling. Though you are gone, you still speak to my heart.

*Roy Croft, "Love," *The Best Loved Poems of the American People*, Hazel Felleman, ed. (Garden City, NY: Doubleday, 1936), p. 25.

OUTPOURINGS
OF COMFORT

"By faith Abel offered unto God a more excellent sacrifice than Cain, by which he obtained witness that he was righteous, God testifying of his gifts: and by it he being dead yet speaketh."
—*Hebrews 11:4*

"That their hearts might be comforted, being knit together in love." —*Colossians 2:2*

"What doth the LORD thy God require of thee, but to fear the LORD thy God, to walk in all his ways, and to love him, and to serve the LORD thy God with all thy heart and with all thy soul." —*Deuteronomy 10:12*

"And I heard a voice from heaven saying unto me, Write, Blessed are the dead which die in the Lord from henceforth: Yea, saith the Spirit, that they may rest from their labors; and their works do follow them." —*Revelation 14:13*

"Keep yourselves in the love of God, looking for the mercy of our Lord Jesus Christ unto eternal life." —*Jude 21*

"And now these three remain: faith, hope and love. But the greatest of these is love." —*1 Corinthians 13:13 (NIV)*

SECTION THREE

NEEDING HELP

NEEDING HELP

OUTPOURINGS OF GRIEF

I'm facing eye surgery, Lord.

I must maintain my independence
And be able to drive.

It's not the surgery I fear, Lord,
But my need for someone's help.

What shall I do? (If only my beloved were here.)
The children live quite far away.
Not one is free to come and stay
When there is no emergency.
My close friend further up the state
Has responsibilities and cannot come.

Who is there to help?

Two friends who live nearby have offered to help.
(I was too proud to ask.)
Are they Your answer to my prayer?
Did You prompt them, Lord?

Humbly, gratefully,
I accept Your help through them.
Let me, in turn, Lord, be the friend
You use to meet some other person's need.

OUTPOURINGS
OF COMFORT

"Your Father knoweth what things ye have need of, before ye ask him." —*Matthew 6:8*

"But my God shall supply all your need according to his riches in glory by Christ Jesus."
—*Philippians 4:19*

"Let us therefore come boldly unto the throne of grace, that we may obtain mercy, and find grace to help in time of need." —*Hebrews 4:16*

"Then helped every one his neighbor; and every one said to his brother, Be of good courage."
—*Isaiah 41:6*

"Inasmuch as ye have done it unto one of the least of these my brethren, ye have done it unto me."
—*Matthew 25:40*

My Outpourings

MONEY!

OUTPOURINGS OF GRIEF

Why should money haunt me so?
Bills keep coming in,
Draining my resources.
The future looks bleak;
The economy, so weak.

What if I live another thirty years?

What if I have a major illness?
What if I become helpless
And need to be in a nursing home?
What if I become a burden to the children?

I must let go of the what-ifs and the tomorrows?
I must read Thy Word and consider?
Consider what, Lord?

Consider the lilies,
Manna from heaven,
The loaves and fishes,
The coin with Caesar's image,
The widow's mite.

Your vast treasures
Will more than meet my every need.
And, in love, I am to give a generous portion
Back to Thee?

Then teach me,
One day at a time, Lord,
To look to Thee for my needs
(Not my wants!)
To accept Your daily provision
With gratitude and love
And to seek Your ways
For me to share with others.

OUTPOURINGS
OF COMFORT

"And why take ye thought for raiment? Consider the lilies of the field, how they grow; they toil not, neither do they spin." —*Matthew 6:28*

"Therefore take no thought, saying, What shall we eat? or, What shall we drink? or, Wherewithal shall we be clothed? . . . for your heavenly Father knoweth that ye have need of all these things. But seek ye first the kingdom of God, and his righteousness; and all these things shall be added unto you." —*Matthew 6:31–33*

"But my God shall supply all your need according to his riches in glory by Christ Jesus."
—*Philippians 4:19*

"For we brought nothing into this world, and it is certain we can carry nothing out. And having food and raiment, let us be therewith content."
—*1 Timothy 6:7–8*

My Outpourings

_____

_____

_____

_____

_____

_____

_____

_____

_____

_____

_____

_____

_____

_____

_____

_____

_____

_____

_____

_____

_____

WHAT ABOUT MY RINGS?

OUTPOURINGS OF GRIEF

Lord, many of my widow friends
Have put their wedding rings away
Or have had them made into new jewelry.
Their commitment was "till death us do part,"
they say. I respect their decision.

My rings retain their same familiar place;
They're still a part of me.
Symbolically, they sealed our commitment
To each other.

I remember your words, my dear,
When you slipped the engagement ring
Upon my finger.
You were still a college student then,
Struggling financially.

"Some of the money,
I earned by singing at weddings," you said.
"In our life together, we shall have great joy!
Some of the money, I earned by singing for funerals.
We shall know sorrow, too.
Most of it I earned by serving
As minister of music at church.
We shall spend our life together serving God."

My simple, matching wedding band
Was lovingly placed upon my finger
At our wedding,
Where you sang "Because" to me,
And the soloist prayerfully sang,
"Seal us, O Holy Spirit. Seal us for service today."

Our lives are still sealed in my heart, dear;
And my rings are precious symbols of our love.
I cannot part with them.

The small diamond still sparkles,
And my wedding band, though somewhat worn,
feels comfortable where it has always been.
I look at them and remember
Joy,
Sorrow,
Service,
Love!

OUTPOURINGS
OF COMFORT

"And the LORD God said, It is not good that the man should be alone; I will make him a help meet for him. . . . Therefore shall a man leave his father and his mother, and shall cleave unto his wife: and they shall be one flesh." —*Genesis 2:18, 24*

"Wives, submit yourselves unto your own husbands, as it is fit in the Lord. Husbands, love your wives." —*Colossians 3:18–19*

"Live joyfully with the wife whom thou lovest." —*Ecclesiastes 9:9*

"Thou feedest them with the bread of tears; and givest them tears to drink in great measure."
—*Psalm 80:5*

"We are laborers together with God."
—*1 Corinthians 3:9*

"As for me and my house, we will serve the LORD." —*Joshua 24:15*

"And now abide[s] . . . love."
—*1 Corinthians 13:13 (NKJV)*

HANDLES FOR HELPING

OUTPOURINGS OF GRIEF

My dear,
What if death were reversed
And I had died first?

You would have grieved, yes;
But you would have continued
With your work of helping others—
Young people, through Christian education,
And multitudes, through your gift of music.

Your handles for service
Would still be in place.
You'd simply continue as before,
Though probably at greater pace.

I have no ready handles now.
My work was that of helping you,
And the door is closed forever.

Where are my handles now, Lord?
Please show me fresh new ways
That I can help others
And thus serve Thee.

OUTPOURINGS
OF COMFORT

"Having then gifts differing according to the grace that is given to us, whether . . . ministry, let us wait on our ministering; or he that teacheth, on teaching; or he that exhorteth, on exhortation. . . . serving the Lord . . . continuing instant in prayer; distributing to the necessity of saints; given to hospitality." —*Romans 12:6–8,11–13*

"A man's gift maketh room for him."
—*Proverbs 18:16*

"All the widows stood by him [Peter] weeping, and showing the coats and garments which Dorcas made, while she was with them." —*Acts 9:39*

"Ye also helping together by prayer for us."
—*2 Corinthians 1:11*

"And on the sabbath we went out of the city by a river side, where prayer was wont to be made; and we sat down, and spake unto the women which resorted thither." —*Acts 16:13*

"So when they had dined, Jesus saith to Simon Peter, Simon, son of Jona, lovest thou me more than these? He saith unto him, Yea, Lord; thou knowest that I love thee. He saith unto him, Feed my lambs." —*John 21:15*

"Go home to thy friends, and tell them how great things the Lord hath done for thee, and hath had compassion on thee." —*Mark 5:19*

My Outpourings

LONELINESS AND SELF-PITY

OUTPOURINGS OF GRIEF

Loneliness engulfs me, Lord.
I miss my beloved husband!

I miss our busy life together.
I miss the fun and fellowship we shared.
I miss his undergirding love.
I miss my life partner and best friend.
I've lost so much, Lord!

I still have my family, of course,
And I love them dearly.
But I cannot expect them to give me a life.
I must create my own new life.

I refuse to become a recluse,
Wallowing in loneliness and self-pity
In shade-darkened rooms.

Make me to know Thy ways, O Lord,
    to "company with others,"
    to reach out and touch,
    to interact and grow,
    to become a mutual blessing.

Please assuage my loneliness and grief, Lord.

Outpourings of Comfort

"I watch, and am as a sparrow alone upon the housetop." —*Psalm 102:7*

"A man that hath friends must show himself friendly." —*Proverbs 18:24*

"I was glad when they said unto me, Let us go into the house of the Lord." —*Psalm 122:1*

"We took sweet counsel together, and walked unto the house of God in company." —*Psalm 55:14*

"Jesus said, Suffer little children, and forbid them not, to come unto me: for of such is the kingdom of heaven." —*Matthew 19:14*

"God keeps him occupied with gladness of heart." —*Ecclesiastes 5:20 (NIV)*

My Outpourings

As Was
Our Custom

OUTPOURINGS
OF GRIEF

As was our custom—Claude's and mine—
Each Sunday I attend
Early morning worship service
And Sunday school.

In the early service, I worship Thee, Father,
Through prayer, scripture, sermon, and song.
As I sit in church,
I often picture Claude sitting beside me
(And sometimes slipping his arm
Around my shoulder),
Worshiping joyfully,
Singing gloriously,
Praying humbly,
Listening attentively,
And afterwards, warmly greeting church family.

Then we'd go to Sunday school.
How he loved it!
He played the piano
In his department's opening assembly
(Singing as he played!)
And then actively participated
In the men's Bible class,
Where discussion of Scripture
Was welcomed and encouraged.
He often shared with me
Something of the overflow
Of that morning's experience.

Claude made time, too, in his busy life
As college president
To serve as a deacon in the church.

Thy Church, O Lord, was the focus
Of our faith in Thee,

Our love for Thee,
And our ministry outreach for Thee.
It is still true for me now.

For a long while, I sat alone in church;
But now several of us from our Sunday school class
Sit together.
I try to worship, Father, in spirit and in truth.
I still can't bear to sing, though,
For music touches my heart too deeply.

Our ladies' Sunday school class
Has become my support group
As we study Thy Word,
Pray for each other,
Enjoy Christian fellowship,
And reach out in loving ministry.

Thank You, Father, for Thy Church—
The Body of Christ—
Where I can continue to worship, to serve, and to
grow.

OUTPOURINGS
OF COMFORT

"Serve the LORD with gladness: come before his
presence with singing." —*Psalm 100:2*

"Let us not give up meeting together, as some are in the habit of doing, but let us encourage one another—and all the more as you see the Day approaching." —*Hebrews 10:23–25 (NIV)*

"It was too painful for me; until I went into the sanctuary of God; then understood I their end." —*Psalm 73:16–17*

"I have seen you in the sanctuary and beheld your power and your glory. Because your love is better than life, my lips will glorify you. I will praise you as long as I live." —*Psalm 63:2–4 (NIV)*

"For though I be absent in the flesh, yet am I with you in the spirit, joying and beholding your order, and the steadfastness of your faith in Christ." —*Colossians 2:5*

WHERE DO I BEGIN?

OUTPOURINGS OF GRIEF

I'm ready to reach out to others, Lord.
But how do I begin? And where?

Find a "near edge," my daughter.

That sounds familiar, Father.
Claude and I often spoke of "near edges"
For mission opportunity, but it seems so long ago.
I had almost forgotten our favorite quote:
    "Reach out and touch the near edge of a great need
and act upon it with some degree of sacrifice."*

Where are my near edges now, Father?

All around you, daughter!
Great needs are everywhere.
Begin with your neighbors.

My neighbors, Lord?
The two hundred families
In our residential development?
But we hardly know each other.
Life is impersonal here.

Get to know them one by one.
Many are hurting and need a word of comfort.
Some are lonely and need a word of cheer.
Others are sick and need a helping hand.
Some are struggling
With family problems and relationships
And need your prayers.

Then prayer is my starting point—my *near edge*!
I shall first reach out to them in loving prayer!
Then, as I get to know them personally,
Help me not to pry or judge,
But to love and affirm.

And as their needs unfold,
Help me serve my neighbor
As if I were serving Thee.

Are there other "near edges" too, Father?

Widows, Lord? Like me?
I am to help minister to new widows,
Beginning with those in my Sunday School class?
But I am weak
And not a good example for other widows.

But you understand something of their hurt.
You, too, have suffered loss.
Tell them so. Encourage them.

Then use me in Thy will and purpose, Lord.
Show me the "near edges"
Where You want me to serve.

*(From *Include Me Out!* by Colin Morris)

OUTPOURINGS
OF COMFORT

"And the LORD turned the captivity of Job, when he prayed for his friends." —*Job 42:10*

"Pure religion and undefiled before God and the Father is this, To visit the fatherless and widows in their affliction, and to keep himself unspotted from the world." —*James 1:27*

"They helped every one his neighbor; and every one said to his brother, Be of good courage." —*Isaiah 41:6*

"And this commandment have we from him, That he who loveth God love his brother also." —*1 John 4:21*

"[God] who comforteth us in all our tribulation, that we may be able to comfort them which are in any trouble, by the comfort wherewith we ourselves are comforted of God." —*2 Corinthians 1:4*

"But I [Christ Jesus] have prayed for thee [Peter], that thy faith fail not: and when thou art converted, strengthen thy brethren." —*Luke 22:32*

WALKING

OUTPOURINGS OF GRIEF

I'm learning to *walk*, my dear.
It's good therapy,
Not only for physical aches and pain
But also for my wounded soul.

I walk around the neighborhood,
Mornings and evenings, too.
I'm seeing God's world through eyes
Fresh-washed with tears.
Grass and plants are glorious shades of green.
Tropical flowers spatter-paint the shrubs.
Stately palms climb skyward.
Sunrises and sunsets
Watercolor heavenly backdrops.
Rainbows caress the sky.
Busy birds swoop and sing.
Soft brown rabbits scurry about.

Why didn't I notice these before?

I meet neighbors as I walk
And make new friends.
I meet their children and learn their names.
I learn the names of neighbors' pets, too!
They are expanding my little world.

And as I walk, I pray and sing.
I don't sing aloud ('twould be a dreadful sound!)
But in my mind the words and melody
Ring pure and sweet.
How the hymns have blessed!
  Does Jesus Care?
  Just When I Need Him
  Jesus Is All the World to Me
  All the Way My Savior Leads Me
  I've Found a Friend
  I Am Thine, O Lord

Have Thine Own Way
Great Is Thy Faithfulness
He Leadeth Me
Blessed Assurance
It Is Well With My Soul
Amazing Grace
Blessed Redeemer
Trust and Obey
Yes, I'm learning to
"Walk with the Lord in the light of His Word,"
Right here where I am!
And oh, "what a glory He sheds on my way"
As I learn to trust Him more
And to obey.

Outpourings of Comfort

"He hath showed thee, O man, what is good; and
what doth the LORD require of thee, but to do
justly, and to love mercy, and to walk humbly with
thy God?" —*Micah 6:8*

"Cause me to know the way wherein I should walk;
for I lift up my soul unto thee." —*Psalm 143:8*

"As ye have therefore received Christ Jesus the Lord, so walk ye in him." —*Colossians 2:6*

"And walk in love, as Christ also hath loved us." —*Ephesians 5:2*

"Be filled with the Spirit; speaking to yourselves in psalms and hymns and spiritual songs, singing and making melody in your heart to the Lord." —*Ephesians 5:18–19*

"But they that wait upon the LORD shall renew their strength; they shall mount up with wings as eagles; they shall run, and not be weary; and they shall walk, and not faint." —*Isaiah 40:31*

"But if we walk in the light, as he is in the light, we have fellowship one with another." —*1 John 1:7*

MY SOCIAL LIFE

OUTPOURINGS OF GRIEF

Like other changes in my life, Father,
My social life has changed drastically, too.
Now that I'm alone,
Most of our couple-friends
Have distanced themselves.
A precious few still include me in their circle.

I understand.
We have little in common now.
Claude and I were like that—
Too busy with each other
And other couples
To invite widows into our joy-filled lives.

With loving gratitude for their friendship,
I release all couple-friends
Who wish to drop out of my life.

I rejoice with them
That they still have each other to cherish.

Who are my friends now, Father?
The many who have been faithful friends
Through the years (priceless gifts from Thee!),
The new widow friends I've made
Since Claude's death,
My church friends and neighborhood friends,
And the yet-undiscovered friends
Out there in my future—
Waiting for our lives to touch and bless.
Lead us to each other, Father.
Please help me be a true friend.

Lord Jesus, You are my greatest friend!
You promised that You would never leave me
Nor forsake me.
I'm truly blest!

Outpourings of Comfort

"My friends and companions avoid me because of my wounds." —*Psalm 38:11 (NIV)*

"Go home to thy friends, and tell them how great things the Lord hath done for thee, and hath had compassion on thee." —*Mark 5:19*

"A man that hath friends must show himself friendly: and there is a friend that sticketh closer than a brother." —*Proverbs 18:24*

"I have called you friends; for all things that I have heard of my Father I have made known unto you." —*John 15:15*

"He hath said, I will never leave thee, nor forsake thee." —*Hebrews 13:5*

My Outpourings

SECTION FOUR

COUNTING MY BLESSINGS

COUNTING MY BLESSINGS

OUTPOURINGS OF GRIEF

Father, I've counted only my losses
Since Claude's death;
I've failed to count my blessings.
Self-pity put blinders on my eyes.
Please forgive me.

You showed Your love for me
Through Christ's life and death and resurrection.
Thank You for my salvation.

You blessed me with Claude's loving presence
For thirty-nine years of marriage.
Thank You for my beloved husband.

You gave us three wonderful children,
Two sons and a daughter,
Who are now responsible adults.

Busy with their own lives,
But not too busy for me.
Thank You for our children.

You are blessing us with grandchildren, too—
Four precious granddaughters thus far—
With healthy, growing minds and bodies.
Thank You for our grandchildren.

You gave us loving parents, Claude's and mine,
Who not only loved us but affirmed us
And helped in many ways.
Thank You for our parents.

You gave us friends
To enrich our lives in countless ways.
Thank You for our friends.

You provided for all our needs.

You gave us work to do that honored You.
Light for each dark road,
Laughter to lighten the load,
Strength for crisis times,
Forgiveness and peace,
And Your love at all times.
I know that You will bless my future, too!
Thank You, Father, for Your faithfulness.
I'm rich indeed!

Outpourings
of Comfort

"Be ye thankful." —*Colossians 3:15*

"I will praise the name of God with a song, and will magnify him with thanksgiving."
—*Psalm 69:30*

"Bless the LORD, O my soul, and forget not all his benefits: who forgiveth all thine iniquities; who healeth all thy diseases; who redeemeth thy life from destruction; who crowneth thee with lovingkindness and tender mercies; who satisfieth thy mouth with good things." —*Psalm 103:2–5*

"I thank my God upon every remembrance of you." —*Philippians 1:3*

"Enter into his gates with thanksgiving, and into his courts with praise." —*Psalm 100:4*

MY OUTPOURINGS

_____

_____

_____

_____

_____

_____

_____

_____

_____

_____

_____

THY PEACE

OUTPOURINGS OF GRIEF

You are my peace, Lord Jesus.
Your love enfolds me and calms my grief.

You've wept with me in my loss.
You've listened patiently to my outbursts.
You've guided me through the wilderness.
You've opened to me the Scriptures
And encouraged me to claim Your promises.

You've kept Your promises, Lord:
The promise of forgiveness,
The Holy Spirit's help,
Comfort,
Rest,
Courage,
Strength,
Peace.

You've shown me,
By Your own example in Gethsemane,
That the Father's will is best.
Someone has said,
  "God's will: Exactly what I would choose
  if I knew all the facts."
I don't know all the facts, Lord Jesus, but *You* do.
And *You* chose God's will
Even when it meant death.

I relinquish my selfish claims
Upon my beloved husband.
(His love was a grace gift from God!)
I relinquish the plans we'd made
For our golden years of retirement.
(I'm grateful for the thirty-nine wonderful years
We were together!)
Humbly, I accept God's higher wisdom
Within the circumstances of Claude's death.

Lord, You had already prepared a place for him,
Even as You had promised;
And I shall join him there in God's time.

I trust You.
I love You.
Thank You for Your gift of peace, Lord Jesus.

Outpourings
of Comfort

"For he is our peace." —*Ephesians 2:14*

"These things I have spoken unto you, that in me
ye might have peace." —*John 16:33*

"Peace I leave with you, my peace I give unto you:
not as the world giveth, give I unto you. Let not
your heart be troubled, neither let it be afraid."
—*John 14:27*

"And the peace of God, which passeth all understanding, shall keep your hearts and minds
through Christ Jesus." —*Philippians 4:7*

"And he [Jesus] went a little further [in Gethsemane], and fell on his face, and prayed, saying, O my Father, if it be possible, let this cup pass from me: nevertheless, not as I will, but as thou wilt." —*Matthew 26:39*

"Thy will be done in earth." —*Matthew 6:10*

"Now may the Lord of peace himself give you peace at all times and in every way." —*2 Thessalonians 3:16 (NIV)*

"And as they thus spake, Jesus himself stood in the midst of them, and saith unto them, Peace be unto you." —*Luke 24:36*

THY WILL, THY
WAY, THY TIME

OUTPOURINGS
OF GRIEF

Thy will?
Father, was death at sixty-two
A part of Your perfect will for Claude's life?
Did You plan everything from the beginning?
Had he completed Your purpose
For his earthly life?
Having finished his work,
Did he die in Your way and time?
I wonder.

Thy way?
Father, did You intentionally create
The circumstances in which he died?
Or did You work lovingly and creatively
For his highest good
Within circumstances
Brought about by life choices—

His and others'?
My heart ponders.

Thy time?
Father, was it really Your scheduled time
For him to die?
You could have intervened
And spared him yet again, but You didn't.

Father, as my frail mind contemplates
Your omnipotence,
I kneel in reverent awe.

My human understanding of Your divine will
Is meager indeed, yet I am confident
That unseen aspects of Your wise and loving will
Prevailed in Claude's death.

I can safely trust You with the unknown.

Claude loved You and trusted You.
So do I.
Thy will, Thy way, Thy time
In my life, too, and in my death.

OUTPOURINGS
OF COMFORT

"The LORD gave, and the LORD hath taken away; blessed be the name of the LORD." —*Job 1:21*

"And he . . . kneeled down, and prayed, saying, Father, if thou be willing, remove this cup from me: nevertheless, not my will, but thine, be done." —*Luke 22:41–42*

"That good, and acceptable, and perfect, will of God." —*Romans 12:2*

"As for God, his way is perfect." —*Psalm 18:30*

"For my thoughts are not your thoughts, neither are your ways my ways, saith the LORD. For as the heavens are higher than the earth, so are my ways higher than your ways, and my thoughts than your thoughts." —*Isaiah 55:8–9*

"I will meditate in thy precepts, and have respect unto thy ways." —*Psalm 119:15*

"All the days ordained for me were written in your book before one of them came to be."
—*Psalm 139:16 (NIV)*

"To everything there is a season, and a time to every purpose under the heaven."
—*Ecclesiastes 3:1*

"Man that is born of a woman is of few days. . . . his days are determined, the number of his months are with thee, thou hast appointed his bounds that he cannot pass." —*Job 14:1, 5*

"My times are in thy hand." —*Psalm 31:15*

HEAVEN

OUTPOURINGS OF GRIEF

I know that you're in heaven, dear.
How wonderful it must be!

A place where God's pure love
Surrounds each one,
Where earth's tears are wiped away,
And joy and praise are everywhere!

Surely there is music there,
And you are singing in heavenly choirs!

You're with Christ, our Savior,
Who led you safely there,
And you're experiencing
The Heavenly Father's love!
Earth-time has ceased to be—
There in eternity!

Have you seen our families, dear?
Are you with your parents now?
Have you seen my mother and father?
And have you met my sister Margaret?
What about your friends who've gone before?

Can you see me now, my dear?
Are you missing me as I miss you?
Or has Heaven filled that void?
Are you burdened for me in my grief?
Please don't grieve for me.
I relinquish you to enjoy heaven
And your great rewards
And to serve God in His new ways
Of ministry and worship.
When your mother was near death,
She kept calling you by name.
And then I heard her sing,
"When we all get to heaven,

What a day of rejoicing that will be.
When we all see Jesus . . . "
(I'd never heard her sing before!)
Was that your answer
To her plea for help with dying?
How like you to speak through music!
Please sing to me!
My earth-years will pass
And our spirits reunite,
For love is eternal and does not die.
I'll see you in heaven, dear!

OUTPOURINGS OF COMFORT

"In my Father's house are many mansions: if it were not so, I would have told you. I go to prepare a place for you. And if I go and prepare a place for you, I will come again, and receive you unto myself; that where I am, there ye may be also." —John 14:2–3

"Eye hath not seen, nor ear heard . . . the things which God hath prepared for them that love him." —1 Corinthians 2:9

"And Jesus said unto him, Verily I say unto thee, Today shalt thou be with me in paradise."
—*Luke 23:43*

"And I saw a new heaven and a new earth: for the first heaven and the first earth were passed away."
—*Revelation 21:1*

"And God shall wipe away all tears from their eyes." —*Revelation 7:17*

"Ye have in heaven a better and an enduring substance." —*Hebrews 10:34*

"The throne of God and of the Lamb shall be in it, and his servants shall serve him: and they shall see his face." —*Revelation 22:3–4*

DO YOU WANT TO BE HEALED?

OUTPOURINGS OF GRIEF

Almost five years have passed, My daughter,
And you are grieving still.
Do you want to be healed?

I'm not sure, Father,
Just what healing means.

If healing means
Forgetting my beloved,
Setting memories aside,
And stepping fearlessly
Into single life again,
Then, no, I don't want to be healed.
I'd rather endure grief's pain.

But if healing means
Consciously choosing the new life

You envision for me now,
Instead of continuing to grieve
For all that I have lost;
And if the future You have planned
Allows me to cherish my love for Claude
And his love for me
And to anticipate joining him in heaven;
And if it opens up ways to serve my fellowman
And to grow as a person,
Then I want to be healed
So that I can move ahead with my life.

Please take away the intense hurt, Lord,
And mend my broken heart.

I embrace my future, Father!
Gently guide me in the way that I should go
As each new day unfolds in Thy will.
I trust You all the way.

I can see now that my painful journey
Through the wilderness of grief
Is leading me to Your promised Canaan land,
Where I shall find
A meaningful life for myself as a widow.

OUTPOURINGS OF COMFORT

"When Jesus saw him . . . he saith unto him, Wilt thou be made whole?" —*John 5:6*

"And he laid his hands on every one of them, and healed them." —*Luke 4:40*

"Behold, I will do a new thing; now it shall spring forth; shall ye not know it? I will even make a way in the wilderness, and rivers in the desert." —*Isaiah 43:19*

"But the land, whither ye go to possess it, is a land of hills and valleys, and drinketh water of the rain of heaven: a land which the LORD thy God careth for: the eyes of the LORD thy God are always upon it, from the beginning of the year even unto the end of the year." —*Deuteronomy 11:11–12*

"But the God of all grace, who hath called us unto his eternal glory by Christ Jesus, after that ye have suffered a while, make you perfect, stablish, strengthen, settle you." —*1 Peter 5:10*

"Wherefore, let them that suffer according to the will of God commit the keeping of their souls to him in well doing, as unto a faithful Creator." —*1 Peter 4:19*

"Go forward." —*Exodus 14:15*

MY OUTPOURINGS

YOUR FUTURE FOR ME, FATHER

OUTPOURINGS OF GRIEF

This future that You've planned for me, Father—
Will it bring happiness?
There will be joy, My daughter,
And joy is better than happiness.

Is there more sorrow still ahead, Father?
Pain and suffering too?
Life—even your bright future, My child—
Exempts no mortal from sorrow, pain, and suffering.

How long must I be mortal, Father?
You cannot know or understand eternity's timetable.
It reveals itself one earth-day at a time.
Trust Me.

Will my sorrow over losing Claude ever cease,
Father?

Not completely, My daughter.
Some of it remains to hold
A special place in your heart for your beloved.
But the pain will diminish;
The memories will bless;
And your life will become more receptive
To the joys I have for you in your future.

Will I still have peace, Father?
Yes, My daughter.
Already, you have experienced My peace
Through Christ, your Savior and Lord.
Abide in Him.
He is your peace.
Follow Him.
He is the way.
Do not fear your future, My daughter.
Christ is with you always.

How will I spend time in my future, Father?
Will I stay actively busy or be helplessly idle?
Don't let busy-ness obsess you, My child.
Being and becoming
Are far more important than doing.
Whatever the circumstances might be,
Work creatively with Me to redeem the time.

OUTPOURINGS
OF COMFORT

"LORD, make me to know mine end, and the measure of my days." —*Psalm 39:4*

"It is not for you to know the times or the seasons, which the Father hath put in his own power." —*Acts 1:7*

"Being confident of this very thing, that he which hath begun a good work in you will perform it until the day of Jesus Christ." —*Philippians 1:6*

"Jesus saith unto him, I am the way, the truth, and the life: no man cometh unto the Father, but by me." —*John 14:6*

"Now the God of peace . . . make you perfect in every good work to do his will, working in you that which is well-pleasing in his sight, through Jesus Christ; to whom be glory for ever and ever. Amen." —*Hebrews 13:20–21*

"In everything by prayer and supplication with thanksgiving let your requests be made known unto God. And the peace of God, which passeth all understanding, shall keep your hearts and minds through Christ Jesus." —*Philippians 4:6–7*

"And, lo, I am with you alway, even unto the end of the world. Amen." —*Matthew 28:20*

"Be thou faithful unto death, and I will give thee a crown of life." —*Revelation 2:10*

YESTERDAY, TODAY, TOMORROW

OUTPOURINGS
OF GRIEF

Today is the tomorrow I embraced yesterday
In Thy will, Father.

I'm now living in the future
Which You have planned for me—
My future, which I welcomed in a conscious act
Of love and trust.

I have turned the corner in my grief.
My life is no longer buried
In the past with my beloved.
Claude's love will go with me always—
Now and forever.
I'm open to my new life as a widow,
Ready to move beyond
This valley of the shadow
Of my beloved husband's death,

Ready to walk—with growing confidence—
In this new direction
In which You are leading me.

Not afraid to walk alone,
For You are with me.
Not afraid to be my own self,
For You are still shaping my personhood.
Not afraid to make mistakes,
For You can redeem them.
Not afraid to lavish love
And encouragement and hope
Upon those whose lives I touch,
For You can nurture every seed I plant.

I want to live my present in Thy presence, Lord.
Please help me abide in Thee,
For Thy love can illumine and bless
Each moment of my life.

OUTPOURINGS
OF COMFORT

"I delight to do thy will, O my God."
—*Psalm 40:8*

"Fear thou not; for I am with thee: be not dismayed; for I am thy God: I will strengthen thee; yea, I will help thee; yea, I will uphold thee with the right hand of my righteousness."
—*Isaiah 41:10*

"Let us run with patience the race that is set before us, looking unto Jesus the author and finisher of our faith." —*Hebrews 12:1–2*

"In all thy ways acknowledge him, and he shall direct thy paths." —*Proverbs 3:6*

"The LORD shall preserve thy going out and thy coming in from this time forth, and even forevermore." —*Psalm 121:8*

"Ye shall go out with joy, and be led forth with peace." —*Isaiah 55: 12*

"What doth the LORD require of thee, but to do justly, and to love mercy, and to walk humbly with thy God?" —*Micah 6:8*

"The joy of the LORD is your strength." —*Nehemiah 8:10*

MY OUTPOURINGS

_____

_____

_____

_____

_____

_____

_____

_____

_____

_____

_____

GIFTING EACH OTHER

OUTPOURINGS OF GRIEF

During our life together, my dear, you encouraged us to gift each other with some personal endeavor to "grow a finer self." This experience enriched our marriage. Our personal-endeavor gifts ranged from simple accomplishments such as preparing a special food, to difficult ones such as gaining a new skill, pursuing a new hobby, overcoming an obstacle, creating original music, writing a book, or fulfilling a dream.

I remember some of your special gifts to me:
Setting my favorite love poem to music,
Taking harp lessons,
Recording your first album,
Preparing gourmet delicacies
(which you named for me),
Compiling a cookbook,

Writing children's songs together,
Conducting the ceremony of placing your
newly-earned doctoral hood on me,
Writing your autobiography
and dedicating it to me.

I also remember some of my gifts to you:
Learning to make peanut brittle,
Finding courage to learn to drive after my sister's
death in an automobile accident,
Writing poetry, devotional books, and
children's songs,
Overcoming my fear of speaking before large
church groups,
Becoming a college student again for teacher
certification.

Since your death, my love, I have gifted you with
Flowers for your grave,

Memorial flowers in church,
Contributions to mission offerings,
Gifts to the Claude Rhea Scholarship Fund,
And contributions to other memorial funds
honoring you.

Now I want to continue
Our tradition of gifting each other
With some personal endeavor
"To grow a finer self."
Perhaps I can begin with this book
About my grief in losing you, my love.
I dedicate it to you.

I want to grow a finer self,
Even through the agony of grief.
Later on, I'll try to finish
My Spoken English Enhancement program
And my book about American Humor.
You encouraged me all the way!

Thank You, Heavenly Father,
For gifting us with such great
Love for each other—love that kept us growing!

OUTPOURINGS
OF COMFORT

"But covet earnestly the best gifts."
—*1 Corinthians 12:31*

"Neglect not the gift that is in thee."
—*1 Timothy 4:14*

"Add to your faith virtue; and to virtue, knowledge."
—*2 Peter 1:5*

"Thou shalt love the Lord thy God with all thy heart . . . and with all thy mind." —*Luke 10:27*

"But grow in grace, and in the knowledge of our Lord and Savior Jesus Christ." —*2 Peter 3:18*

"Every good gift and every perfect gift is from above, and cometh down from the Father."
—*James 1:17*

TEARDROPS:
EVERLASTING JOY

OUTPOURINGS
OF GRIEF

My love, how can it be
That I no longer think of you
Almost every waking moment
And grieve for your loving presence?

There are small spaces of time
When my life is so absorbed in present living
That you are not in my thoughts at all.
How unthinkable!
How sad that I should forget you even for an hour!

But I have not forgotten you, my dear.
You are forever a part of me.
You helped God shape my life
Into my present self.
I carry your love in my heart.
I miss you so very much and always will.

But now I'm caught up in trying to reconstruct
With God's guidance
A meaningful life for myself.
One in which I can help,
Serve, share, learn, love, grow.

I remember the hibiscus plant
We bought at the annual show.
It was called Teardrops,
For several perfectly-shaped white teardrops
Spattered the broad expanse
Of its gorgeous pink blooms.
How we loved it!

Then later, after it had grown much taller,
We saw a different kind of bloom:
Multitudes of small, sturdy, happy pink blossoms
Swaying merrily in the Florida breeze!
Teardrops had been grafted onto a stronger plant!

We named it Everlasting Joy.

Teardrops still bloomed at the lower level,
But as the plant grew ever upward and outward,
Everlasting Joy bloomed in profusion!

Lord Jesus, when teardrops fall,
Help me remember that through faith
I have been grafted in You—
You, the vine;
I, a branch—
Eternally secure in God's love through Thee!
Blessed with Thy fullness of joy on earth
And the promise of everlasting joy in heaven!

Outpourings of Comfort

"I thank my God upon every remembrance of you." —*Philippians 1:3*

"I am come that they might have life, and that they might have it more abundantly."
—*John 10:10*

"I am the vine, ye are the branches. He that abideth in me, and I in him, the same bringeth forth much fruit; for without me ye can do nothing." —*John 15:5*

"Ye shall be sorrowful, but your sorrow shall be turned into joy." —*John 16:20*

"Break forth into joy . . . for the LORD hath comforted his people." —*Isaiah 52:9*

"Everlasting joy shall be unto them." —*Isaiah 61:7*

"I have . . . quieted myself, as a child that is weaned of his mother: my soul is even as a weaned child. Let Israel hope in the LORD from henceforth and for ever." —*Psalm 131:2–3*

"I have you in my heart." —*Philippians 1:7*

OUT OF THE WILDERNESS

OUTPOURINGS OF GRIEF

Father, I no longer want to wander
In the wilderness of grief.

An inner urge is prompting me
To move beyond the darkness of this place
Into Thy light which is ahead.
Make bright the path for me to follow!

Lord Jesus, please walk with me
In this new direction.
Help me follow God's light.

Help me greet each day with gladness,
Which softens sadness
And welcomes the adventure
Of living life abundantly in God's will.

Help me walk in love:
Love for my Heavenly Father,
Love for Thee, my Savior and Lord,
And love for my fellow man.

Let me hold close to my heart
The gift of Claude's love
And the treasured memories
Of our life together.

Help me walk with faith and courage
As I venture further into this new vista
Of my journey.

OUTPOURINGS
OF COMFORT

"Who is this that cometh out of the wilderness."
—*Song of Solomon 3:6*

"And the LORD spake unto me, saying, Ye have compassed this mountain long enough: turn you northward." —*Deuteronomy 2:2–3*

"They wandered in the wilderness in a solitary way . . . their soul fainted in them. Then they cried unto the LORD. . . . And he led them forth by the right way." —*Psalm 107:4–7*

"'For I know the plans I have for you,' declares the LORD, 'plans to prosper you and not to harm you, plans to give you hope and a future.'"
—*Jeremiah 29:11 (NIV)*

"Our fellowship is with the Father, and with his Son Jesus Christ." —*1 John 1:3*

"God is light, and in him is no darkness at all."
—*1 John 1:5*

"And walk in love." —*Ephesians 5:2*

"If we walk in the light, as he is in the light, we have fellowship one with another." —*1 John 1:7*

"This is the day which the LORD hath made; we will rejoice and be glad in it." —*Psalm 118:24*

"Ye shall go out with joy, and be led forth in peace." —*Isaiah 55:12*

MY OUTPOURINGS

_____

_____

_____

_____

_____

_____

_____

_____

_____

HELP, LORD!

OUTPOURINGS
OF GRIEF

I'm well into my future, Father.
I'm now living in the seventh year
Following Claude's death.

Much of the time I'm cheerful, courageous,
Confident, caring, and content,
As I enjoy my children and grandchildren,
My friends and relatives,
And as I try to reach out to widows and students
And to deepen my ministry of prayer.

But at times sorrow shrouds me like a mist,
Obscuring light and joy,
Reminding me only of loss.
I'm still crippled without Claude.
Is grief unending, Father?

These days must come, My child.
Rest quietly and trustingly in My love.

But after you have rested, rise!
Let Christ lead you onward
Through every painful encounter
With recurring grief and discouragement.
He is the Way.
Lean on Him. He cares.

Be at peace.
This too shall pass, and joy will come again.
Keep moving toward the light.

I love you, My daughter.

I love You, too, my Father.
And I trust You.

OUTPOURINGS
OF COMFORT

"Help, LORD." —*Psalm 12:1*

"My heart is sore pained within me." —*Psalm 55:4*

"Rest in the LORD, and wait patiently for him."
—*Psalm 37:7*

"But they that wait upon the LORD shall renew
their strength; they shall mount up with wings as
eagles; they shall run, and not be weary; and they
shall walk, and not faint." —*Isaiah 40:31*

"Jesus saith unto him, I am the way." —*John 14:6*

"And he said unto me, My grace is sufficient for
thee: for my strength is made perfect in weakness."
—*2 Corinthians 12:9*

"I can do all things through Christ which
strengtheneth me." —*Philippians 4:13*

"I will never leave thee, nor forsake thee."
—*Hebrews 13:5*

"I have loved thee with an everlasting love."
—*Jeremiah 31:3*

"Do not cling to events of the past or dwell on what happened long ago. Watch for the new thing I am going to do. It is happening already—you can see it now!" —*Isaiah 43:18–19 (TEV)*

"Rise ye up, take your journey."
—*Deuteronomy 2:24*

MY OUTPOURINGS

GOD'S GRACE IN THE WILDERNESS

OUTPOURINGS OF GRIEF

"The people . . . found grace in the wilderness."
—*Jeremiah 31:2*

Lord God,
Like Thy people, the Israelites,
Wandering in their wilderness long ago,
I, too, found Thy all-sufficient grace
In my wilderness.

Instantly torn asunder from my beloved,
My broken self plummeted into the dark
Wilderness of grief.

But Thy grace—
unmerited divine love and assistance—
encircled me.
Underneath were Your everlasting arms.

Christ my Savior opened up the way
And taught me to walk by faith.
The Holy Spirit consoled me in my sorrow.

Tenderly, You brought me
Through the wilderness of grief,
Blessing me with grace gifts for my journey:
Love,
Comfort,
Forgiveness,
Courage,
Strength,
Hope,
Healing,
Peace.

Heavenly Father,
I love You. I worship You. I praise You!

I pray that other wilderness wanderers
Might find comfort in knowing
That in their wilderness
They, too, can find
Thy wondrous, all-sufficient grace!

OUTPOURINGS OF COMFORT

"The people . . . found grace in the wilderness."
—*Jeremiah 31:2*

"The eternal God is thy refuge, and underneath are the everlasting arms." —*Deuteronomy 33:27*

"For by grace are ye saved through faith; and that not of yourselves: it is the gift of God."
—*Ephesians 2:8*

"And he said unto me, My grace is sufficient for thee: for my strength is made perfect in weakness."
—*2 Corinthians 12:9*

"For we walk by faith, not by sight."
—*2 Corinthians 5:7*

"But the Comforter, which is the Holy Ghost, whom the Father will send in my name, he shall teach you all things, and bring all things to your remembrance, whatsoever I have said unto you." —*John 14:26*

"Let us therefore come boldly unto the throne of grace, that we may obtain mercy, and find grace to help in time of need." —*Hebrews 4:16*

"But the God of all grace, who hath called us unto his eternal glory by Christ Jesus, after that ye have suffered a while, make you perfect, stablish, strengthen, settle you." —*1 Peter 5:10*

"Grace be to you, and peace, from God our Father, and from the Lord Jesus Christ." —*Ephesians 1:2*

"Grow in grace." —*2 Peter 3:18*

POSTLUDE: GROWING IN GRACE

"But grow in grace, and in the knowledge of our Lord and Saviour Jesus Christ. To him be glory both now and for ever. Amen." —*2 Peter 3:18*

At the time I wrote the following poem, "When Life Is Felled," Claude liked it so much that he expressed a fervent desire for it to be read at his funeral someday. Our son, Claude Rhea III, read it at his father's memorial service. My husband's beloved ficus tree, felled by lightning on the day of his death, had become symbolic of his life and of his death.

The poem expresses my heart's desire to keep on growing through Christ my Redeemer, who strengthens me in all of life's circumstances and reminds me of the glorious welcome awaiting us at death!

When Life Is Felled

When life is felled
In Earth's forest,
May its rings reveal
Continuous growth,
Upward toward God
And outward toward my fellowman.

And when death's final process
Transforms life's earthly trunk
Into heavenly scroll,
May Christ my Redeemer
See fit to write thereon:
Thou hast been faithful in the shadows.
Welcome to the light!

My Outpourings